Finding Family

Finding Family

A Reading and Vocabulary Text for Adults

Natalie Hess
Rick Kappra
Laurel Pollard

Ann Arbor
University of Michigan Press

ISBN-13: 978-0-472-03405-5

2014   2013   2012   2011   4   3   2   1

Dedications:

We dedicate this book
> to new immigrants everywhere,
> to hardworking teachers in all lands,
> and to Dr. Gail Weinstein, who has taught us to appreciate the value of our students' stories.

Acknowledgments

We value and respect all of our students whose real experiences have found their way into these stories.

We are grateful to the students at City College of San Francisco for their input.

Thanks to Jackie Newlove, Geneva Hickey, Sonja Franeta, and John Hess for helping us along the way.

Thanks to Kelly Sippell, our editor, who moved us forward in ways that went beyond the call of duty.

Contents

To the Teacher

Welcome to *Finding Family*, a reading and vocabulary text for adult learners of English. Each of the 25 chapters contains a story based on the real-life experiences of immigrant students. The activities that follow each story are designed to:

- help students become engaged, thoughtful, and confident readers
- improve reading competency and fluency
- motivate students to want to read more
- increase vocabulary
- promote lively classroom discussions
- provide models for writing
- assist in building a supportive and engaged learning community.

At the core of the book is a cycle of 25 linked journal entries written by six fictional students in a group in an ESL writing class in Yuma, Arizona. Their teacher, Veronica Garcia, is also an immigrant.

During the course of the book, the students and Veronica all share their challenges and successes. They write about leaving home, war, separation from family, adjusting to a new culture, depression, finding jobs, making new friends, falling in love, and finding new family. These are stories of resilience and surprising twists of fate, of working hard and finding help where you least expect it.

Organization

Preview

The preview provides students an opportunity to get acquainted with their classmates and with the characters in the book

Parts 1-4

- Each part contains six or seven chapters.
- Each part opens with a letter from the teacher of the class, Veronica. In Part 1, this letter serves as the reading for Chapter 1. It is Veronica's initial letter to her class.
- Parts 2, 3, and 4 open with a Letter from Veronica, but these letters serve as the introduction to the part, rather than as a core reading within a chapter. Reading these letters aloud as a class will re-orient students to the flow of the entries and will provide clues as to where the stories are going. Use them to help make sure students are following the events in the book.

- Each part includes a final Checklist to help make students aware of their efforts, their approaches to learning, and their progress.
- Each part ends with a review (described on pages x–xi in Connecting the Chapters.)

Appendixes

- Reflecting on the Story
- Note Taking: Remembering the People and the Stories
- Preview of Words by Chapter
- Common Irregular Verbs

Navigating the Chapters

Vocabulary Preview

To begin each chapter, six vocabulary words are previewed. These words are vocabulary that your students may already be familiar with, which increases the chances that students will be successful making connections between words and/or using the words to make a few predictions about the journal entries. Adult Education classes usually involve a range of students. Although most words are "common" or may be perceived as "easy," a few higher-level words have been included to challenge more advanced students.

Approaches to previewing include:

- **Read and repeat.** Say the words, and ask students to repeat them.
- **Students teach a word.** Ask students to explain any words they know or give examples of the word in a sentence. Call on volunteers, or write the words on the board and invite a few students come up and put their initials by words they know. Ask students who know the words to explain them to students who don't.
- **Briefly explain.** Explain words the students don't know. Consider giving examples, sketching, miming, or offering quick translations.
- **Talk about the illustration.** Whenever possible, relate words to the illustration that appears just above them on the page. Either invite students to try to use words to talk about the illustration, or describe the illustration using the words, to build context for both the words and the journal entry.

Before We Read

Encourage students to talk about the illustration and the title. Prompt them to recall and/or predict information, and to link their personal experience with what they will read.

Scanning

Ask students to look for the answer to the question, write an answer, and then compare their answers.

Journal Entry

The journal entry is the core of each chapter. Approaches to reading it include:

- **Read it aloud.** Ask your students to read along silently.
- **Students read it aloud.** Ask individuals to read paragraphs either for the whole class or in groups.
- **Students read it silently.**
- **Students read it at home.** Encourage them to read without a dictionary the first time.

Help students guess the meanings of unfamiliar words from context, whenever possible. Encourage students to ask questions when they do not understand something.

What Happened?

This is a comprehension activity so it's important to give students time to think and write. Guide them back to appropriate places in the journal entries for answers when necessary. Ask students to discuss their answers using one of the interaction routines on page xii.

Think about It

This activity requires students to make and discuss inferences. Allow sufficient time for students to think. Encourage them to write notes, draw pictures, or chat with partners.

My Experiences

In this discussion activity, students recall the story together and relate incidents and themes from the journal entries to their own experiences. Teach the phrase, "I'd rather not talk about that" and the lighter, "I pass," and give them the option to pass if they wish. They should always be able to choose which questions and topics they want to discuss.

After discussion, ask students to choose a topic from My Experiences to write about in their journals. If your students have little time for homework, give them time in class to write—or at least begin—their journal entries.

Vocabulary—Working with Words

Students deepen their understanding of new words and begin using them. Fill in the Blanks, Word Families, Do I Know These Words? and Categories are exercises that allow students to manipulate and recycle the target vocabulary. You may find it beneficial to have volunteers model one or two items and/or to ask pairs to compare their answers.

Making the Words My Own

These activities take vocabulary learning a step further. Students master new words and use them in personal contexts. Exercise types include Vocabulary Cards, Vocabulary House, Vocabulary Challenge, Finish the Sentence and Use and Remember. These activities will "stretch" students. Encourage all attempts, and help students understand that their "mistakes" are chances to identify where they need help.

Connecting the Chapters

A Letter from Veronica

Veronica, the teacher, writes a brief note to her students at the beginning of each new part and at the end of the book. Her letters will re-orient your students to the flow of the stories and will provide a few details about where the stories are going. They serve as mini-reviews, which can help students in open-enrollment classes catch up.

Veronica's notes are not full chapters; we suggest you simply read them aloud with your students, using them to check to make sure that your students are following the events in the book.

Part Checklist

The final chapter in each part ends with a checklist of some study skills and habits. This is intended to help students become better language learners by making them aware of their efforts, their approaches to learning, and their successes.

Guiding Principles

Finding Family builds a sense of community. Students support each other in their learning and have fun together. When students want to come to class, attendance and student retention improve!

Readings

- are stories because theme, plot, and character engage students, and increase the likelihood that they will remember language they encounter.
- are in journal format to suggest the truth: they are based on the authentic experiences of immigrants to the U.S.—experiences that students can relate to. The journal format also serves as a model for students in their own journal writing.
- are authentic, providing rich opportunities for discussion and writing.

Activities

- are designed to allow students to succeed at their own level of competence in multi-level classes.
- are student-centered, providing the teacher time to observe, coach, think, and breathe while students work.
- provide a context for students to recognize and appreciate the value of their own life experiences
- build community by fostering the sharing of experiences and information among classmates
- create a safe place where students can be active yet need not be in the spotlight.

Vocabulary

Vocabulary is vital for language learning. Students are justly proud when they can remember and use new words. Vocabulary Preview words have been carefully selected with the needs and competencies of Adult Education students in mind. Most are among the most frequently used words in English; some are academic words used across disciplines.

Each chapter of *Finding Family* supports students in three stages of vocabulary learning reflected in Vocabulary Preview, Working with Words, and Making the Words My Own. Our aim is to help students not only learn new words but keep the words they learn. We hope that this sequence of strategies for vocabulary learning will boost your students' success and confidence, increasing their motivation.

Journal Writing

- supports all the other skills: it gives students a head start in thinking about topics they may speak about; it can be used to explore ideas before, during, and after reading; and it's good holistic practice with grammar and vocabulary.
- builds pride and self-confidence because students see their own improvement as writers over time.
- builds classroom community when selected entries are shared in class (as is the case of Veronica's students in the book).
- encourages self-discovery, self-revelation, and self-expression. When people write informally, they often tell more about themselves and in more interesting ways than they do when they speak or engage in more formal types of writing. Teachers who include journaling often find that they are enjoying their students more than ever.

Interaction Routines

When students are actively engaged and interacting, they learn more and remember more. They also have more fun!

Activities work best when you use routines that promote student interaction. Most of the activities in *Finding Family* are pair or group work, but students can also do them on their own. For example, you might try first letting students do an activity on their own, then share ideas with a partner, and finally bring their suggestions to a group or to the whole class. Many activities can also be done as whole-class mingles.

Here are some Interaction Routines that you can use with activities in *Finding Family*.

- **Pair Share.** Before speaking or writing, students in pairs talk and listen to each other. Partners raise their hands together when they have both practiced their answer.
- **Mingle.** Students stand up. They approach one classmate at a time and talk about the assigned topic. After they have talked to a few classmates, they return to their seats.
- **Small Group Work.** Sitting in small groups, students talk and listen to each other.
- **Write Before You Speak.** Students get ready to speak by writing—or drawing— some ideas first. Then they talk with classmates.
- **Exercise Correction Routine.** In pairs or trios, students compare the work they have done. They raise their hands if they can't agree or need help.

Two Final Notes

1. Our students have rich and varied lives. We believe in giving them opportunities to discuss their own experiences **when and if they choose**. Some topics that may be sensitive for some students are the very ones that other students most enjoy discussing. Make clear to your students that in this class they go only as far into their personal lives as they choose to. Always give them the option to pass.

2. In many exercises, more than one good answer is possible. This is by design. Encourage discussion!

Online Resources

Teachers will find additional activities online at www.press.umich.edu/esl/tm/. All can be printed and copied to supplement this book.

To the Student

Welcome to *Finding Family!*

This book is about six students in an ESL writing class. They are finding new homes and making new friends. They are learning how to get along on their jobs and in their communities while using their new language. They are exploring their new lives.

We hope you will enjoy reading, writing, and talking about these students. This will help you to talk and write about yourselves and learn a lot of English.

Here are some ideas to help you learn English and become a better language learner using *Finding Family*:

- Work with a partner or a group in class and outside of class. It makes learning more interesting and more fun.
- Ask questions when you don't understand something. You can ask your teacher, or you can ask a classmate.
- Keep a journal. You can write whatever you want in your journal. We suggest some topics in Finding Family.
- Do something to remember new words. *Finding Family* offers many different ways to do this. And you can share your own ideas for learning words with your teacher and classmates.
- Review what you study in class when you get home. Even if you review for only a few minutes, it will help you remember.
- Have fun! Learning a new language is not easy, but you can have fun with your classmates and your teacher as you learn.

If you want to tell us how you feel about learning English together with the students who are *Finding Family*, we would be very happy to hear from you at esladmin@umich.edu.

Best wishes,

Natalie Hess
Rick Kappra
Laurel Pollard

Preview
Getting to Know Each Other

Your Book

The title of this book is *Finding Family*. Take a quick look through the book.

1. What do you think "finding family" means?
2. What do you think the stories in this book will be about?

Your Class

Meeting Your Classmates

Complete the chart about your classmates. Walk around and ask *What's your name? Where are you from? What are your hobbies or interests?* Write your own topic in the last column.

Name	Country	Interests or hobbies	_____

Share Your Information

Talk about the people you spoke to. Create a class profile to show how many men and women are in the class. Make a poster or show information about your class in some other type of graphic.

Thinking about Your Class

What makes a good class? Write two ideas here:

_____   _____

In small groups, talk about your ideas. Tell the whole class.

Veronica and Her Writing Class

Veronica Lopez' writing class has 30 students. They are in several writing groups. These six students are the people you will meet in this book. Just like you, they are trying to learn English. They have plenty of problems, but they have a lot of fun, too.

Lydia Gonzales
Mexico, age 18

Ernesto Rodriguez
Mexico, age 20

Christina Evans
Bosnia, age 23

Veronica Lopez, Teacher
El Salvador, age 42

Fouad Rachmani
Sudan, age 26

Tadeo Nishimura
Japan, age 30

Hamad Al-Thani
Jordan, age 57

1. Do any of the students remind you of someone you know? Write your ideas here.

   _____

   Work with a group. Explain your answers.

2. Look at the Contents. What do you think happens to the students? Tell the class.

3. What do you know about the countries these students come from?

PART 1

All of Us Have Good Stories

1 Veronica Finds Her Story

 Vocabulary Preview

afraid   grade   look forward to   parents   repeat   toys

 Before We Read

1. Talk about the picture. What do you see? What is happening? What do you think will happen next?

2. Talk about the title of the chapter. What do you think Veronica wrote about?

3. Do you remember something that happened when you first went to school? How did you feel?

▷ **Scanning**

Read Veronica's letter fast. Answer the question.

What happened to the chicken? _____

Talk about your answer with a classmate.

Veronica's Letter to Her Class

Read the letter.

Dear Students,

I am Veronica Lopez, your teacher. I hope you are all going to enjoy this class. We are going to read, write, talk, and learn together. You already know a lot of English, but you want to learn more. You told me you want to write better, and you told me you want to read better. So that's what we are going to do. We will read each other's journals and write to each other.

First please tell me a story about something interesting in your life. Here is my story.

I was born in El Salvador. My parents brought me to the United States when I was five years old. When I started school, I didn't know any English. I didn't understand one word. I was afraid to talk, and I was afraid of the teacher. I had no friends. I had to repeat the first grade two times. My second time in the first grade, I made one good friend. Her name was Amelia. She spoke English and Spanish because her dad was Mexican and her mom was U.S.-American. Amelia spoke Spanish with her dad and English with her mom. Amelia helped me. I started speaking and learning English, and soon I was less afraid of school.

Sometimes I went to Amelia's house to play. Amelia's house had two floors. It was always clean, and there was a lot of nice furniture. There was a big garden behind the house. The grass looked like a beautiful clean carpet. Amelia had her own room, with many books and toys. Her mom was very pretty and had beautiful blond hair. She baked cookies and made delicious dinners. She was like the moms in storybooks.

At my house, things were very different. My dad didn't always have a job. My mom washed clothes for other people. In our house, there were always big piles of dirty clothes. My dad sometimes brought home a live chicken for dinner. After my mother cut off the chicken's head, the chicken ran around without a head. My mother plucked the feathers off the chicken. Sometimes I helped her. Then we had chicken dinner. I didn't invite friends to my house because I didn't want them to see the dirty clothes and chicken feathers.

I thought, "Amelia's life is right! My life is wrong." But then something changed for me. In the fifth grade, Mrs. Bledowski was my teacher. She said, "I want you to write about your life, Veronica. Your life is your story, and you have a good story here! Tell it."

Now you know some of my stories. I look forward to reading yours!

Your teacher,

Veronica

What Happened?

Mark the sentences (T) true or (F) false.

____F____ 1. Veronica is from Mexico.

_____ 2. Veronica spoke English when she started school.

_____ 3. Amelia was Veronica's teacher.

_____ 4. Veronica lived in a big beautiful house.

_____ 5. Veronica felt bad about her house.

_____ 6. Veronica's mother didn't work.

Rewrite the false sentences and make them true. Write them in your notebook.

Think about It

Answer the questions with your group.

1. Why do you think Veronica was afraid of her first grade teacher?

2. Why did Veronica feel her life was "wrong"?

3. Veronica wrote that something changed when she was in the fifth grade. What did she mean?

4. Why did Veronica think that Amelia's life was right and her own life was not right?

5. Highlight or underline a sentence you like in Veronica's letter. Tell why you like this sentence.

↔ My Experiences

Discuss the questions with a partner.

1. Are any of Veronica's experiences similar to any of your experiences?

2. Have you ever felt bad about yourself or about someone in your family?

3. What were your first experiences at school in the United States?

 Choose one of the questions, and write about it in your journal.

abc Vocabulary—Working with Words

Categories

Read the words in the box. Then put the words that go together into groups. You can put a word in more than one group.

enjoy	write	journals	school	English	room	read	chicken
clean	feathers	improve	Spanish	house	better	talk	teacher

<u>Examples</u>

things:	school, chicken, feathers
places:	school, house
words that start with *S*:	school, Spanish
words about school:	teacher, journals, English, write

Share your word groups with the class. Who had the most interesting groups? Take a class vote.

abc Vocabulary—Making the Words My Own

Finish the Sentence

Read the sentences about Veronica with a partner. Look at the underlined words. Find the words in Veronica's letter. Highlight or underline the words in the letter. Then use the words to write about yourself or someone you know.

1. Veronica's <u>parents</u> brought her to the United States when she was five years old.

   My <u>parents</u> _____.

2. Veronica wrote, "Soon I was less <u>afraid of</u> school."

   I am <u>afraid of</u> _____.

3. Veronica <u>repeated</u> the first grade two times.

   I <u>repeated</u> _____.

4. Veronica wrote, "My second time in the first <u>grade</u>, I made one good friend."

   In the first <u>grade</u>, I _____.

5. Amelia had her own room, with many books and <u>toys</u>.

   My favorite <u>toy</u> was _____.

6. Veronica wrote, "I <u>look forward to</u> reading your stories."

   I <u>look forward to</u> _____.

2 Lydia and Ernesto Have a Fight

 Vocabulary Preview

angry   fight   grow up   neighbor   sorry   stupid

 Before We Read

1. Talk about the picture. What do you see? What is happening? What do you think will happen next?

2. Talk about the title of the chapter. What do you think Lydia wrote about?

3. What surprised you about the United States?

▷ **Scanning**

Read Lydia's journal entry fast. Answer the question.

   What is the name of Ernesto's sister? _____

Talk about your answer with a classmate.

Lydia's Journal Entry

Read the journal entry.

Dear Group,

Thank you for your story, Veronica. In my dreams, I see that chicken without a head. It's a good story.

My name is Lydia Gonzales. I come from a little village 80 miles north of Mexico City. Ernesto Rodriguez was my neighbor. He is two years older than I am. Ernesto was always my brother's best friend. He was in our house every day. My mother and Ernesto's mother were best friends, too.

Ernesto's mother often said to my mother, "When Ernesto and Lydia grow up, maybe they will get married." My mother always smiled. Ernesto and I looked at each other. We smiled, too.

Ernesto's family came to the United States first. Before they left, Ernesto told me, "I will wait for you. I love you!" My family came to America a year later. I was 17 years old.

At first we lived in San Diego in an apartment. Ernesto's family lived there, too. I was very happy to see Ernesto again, and he seemed happy to see me, too. But soon he was different. He was not friendly. He seemed "American" to me. One day Ernesto and I had a big fight. We said many angry things to each other.

Ernesto went away to work and study English in Yuma. I missed him very, very much. I was sorry about all the angry things I said to him.

One day I sat down and wrote him a long letter. I told him I was very sorry. I told him I loved him, and then I mailed the letter. When I got home, I met Adriana, Ernesto's sister. She had a letter from Ernesto. Adriana said, "Oh, I'm so sorry to tell you this, Lydia. Ernesto says he's very happy in Yuma. He has an American girlfriend."

I felt so stupid. I wanted to cry. I wanted my letter back, so I ran to the mailbox. The sign on the mailbox was difficult to read. A woman came over and read the sign for me. It said that the mail carrier comes at 5:00 PM. I looked at my watch. It was only 1:00. I was afraid to go away, so I sat down to wait. The time went very, very slowly. I was hungry, but I was afraid to leave. After a long time, it was 2:00. At 3:00 I was very hungry and thirsty, but I stayed by that mailbox. At 5:00 I was sad and tired and still thirsty, but I wasn't hungry any more. There was no mail carrier at 5:00 PM.

The mail carrier finally came at 5:30. She took the mail. She said, "I am very sorry, but I can't give your letter back to you."

❓ What Happened?

Number the sentences in order.

_____ Ernesto's sister tells Lydia that Ernesto has an American girlfriend.

_____ Ernesto moves to Yuma.

_____ Lydia's family move to the U.S.

_____ Ernesto and Lydia live in Mexico.

_____ Ernesto and Lydia have a big fight.

_____ Lydia tries to get her letter back.

_____ Ernesto's family move to the United States.

_____ Lydia writes Ernesto a letter. She says, "I'm sorry. I love you."

_____ Lydia is happy to see Ernesto again.

Copy the sentences in the correct order. Write them in your notebook.

Think about It

Answer the questions in a group.

1. How did Ernesto change?

2. Why did Lydia write to Ernesto?

3. Why did Lydia feel stupid?

4. What might happen next?

←→ My Experiences

Discuss the questions with a partner.

1. Lydia wrote that Ernesto changed after he came to The United States. Did you change after you came here? How?

2. What are some things that happened soon after you came here?

3. Ernesto's best friend was Lydia's brother. Who was your best friend when you were a child? Why were you good friends?

4. Lydia was sorry about things she wrote in her letter. When did you feel sorry about something you did?

5. Lydia had a bad day. Did you ever have a bad day? What happened?

 Choose one of the questions. Write about it in your journal.

abc Vocabulary—Working with Words

Fill in the Blanks

Complete the sentences. Use the words in the box.

angry	fight	grows up	neighbor	sorry	stupid

1. I missed your phone call. I'm _____.

2. Tim forgot Stephanie's birthday. She was very _____.

3. Andrew is only five years old. He wants to be a mail carrier when he _____.

4. We live in Apartment 1C. Our _____ lives in Apartment 1D.

5. The little boys had a _____ They both wanted the ball.

6. Some people think cats are _____, but I think my cat is very smart.

abc Vocabulary—Making the Words My Own
Vocabulary House

1. Draw the rooms of the place where you live or whre you lived before. This will be your Vocabulary House. Choose a home where a lot of things happened to you. Use a big piece of paper. Make the rooms big. Write the name of each room. Don't draw tables, chairs, or other furniture.

2. Choose a word from the Vocabulary Preview. Where does this word go in your Vocabulary House? Write the word in that room. For example, you might write *neighbor* in the kitchen because you often have coffee with your neighbor in the kitchen. Put all of the other words in a room.

3. Tell your classmates about your Vocabulary House. Tell your stories about each word.

4. Keep your Vocabulary House. You can add new words from every chapter and talk with your classmates about them. Your Vocabulary House will help you remember new words. It will help you use the words in new ways.

3 Ernesto Moves to Yuma, Arizona

 ## Vocabulary Preview

clerk	confused	jealous	moved in	tell a lie	woke up

Before We Read

1. Talk about the picture. What do you see? What is happening? What do you think will happen next?

2. Talk about the title of the chapter. What do you think Ernesto wrote about?

3. Why do you think people tell lies?

 ## Scanning

Read Ernesto's journal entry fast. Answer the question.

Where does Fouad work? _____

Talk about your answer with a classmate.

Ernesto's Journal Entry

Read the journal entry.

Dear Group,

I read Lydia's story, and I started laughing. I felt sad and happy at the same time. Lydia's story is also my story. Let me tell you my side of our story. Lydia and I were neighbors in San Diego.

When Lydia's family moved in, I was excited and happy. San Diego became home for me because I could see Lydia again. At first, she was the same Lydia. It was like old times again . . . at first. But there were many boys in the apartments, and all of them wanted to be Lydia's boyfriend. Somali boys wanted to be her boyfriend. Arab boys wanted to be her boyfriend. Mexican and Brazilian boys wanted to be her boyfriend. American boys wanted to be her boyfriend, too. She talked with those boys. I was very jealous. I started having bad dreams. I was angry at Lydia, and Lydia stopped smiling at me. We stopped talking to each other. In my dreams, Lydia married a very handsome American man. In one dream, I fought with that man. I hit him hard. I said to myself, "This is terrible! I'm going crazy. I have to leave San Diego."

I didn't have much money. I went to the bus station. The clerk asked me, "Where do you want to go?" I said, "How far can I go with this money?" He looked confused. Then I remembered my aunt Teresa in Yuma. I always loved Aunt Teresa. I could visit her. I asked the clerk, "Is this enough for a ticket to Yuma?" He said, "Yes."

I came to Yuma in the middle of the night, so I slept in the bus station. In the morning I was very hungry. I went to eat at Tim's Diner. A guy working in the restaurant started talking to me. His name is Fouad Rachmani. He is from Sudan. He helped me find my aunt's apartment. We became friends and roommates, and he helped me find this class. I like it here in Yuma, but I miss my family very much. And I missed Lydia. I wrote a letter to my sister Adriana. Adriana and Lydia are good friends. I told a lie. I wrote, "I have an American girlfriend." I said to myself, "I hope Lydia is jealous now."

? What Happened?

Work with a partner. Answer the questions.

1. Ernesto thought Lydia changed after she moved to San Diego. What change did he see?

   _____

2. Why was Ernesto jealous?

   _____

3. Why did he leave San Diego?

   _____

4. How did Ernesto find his aunt's apartment?

   _____

5. How did Ernesto and Fouad become friends?

   _____

6. Ernesto told Adriana that he had an American girlfriend? Why did he do that?

   _____

 # Think about It

Answer the questions in a group.

1. Why did Ernesto laugh when he read Lydia's journal entry?

2. Why did Ernesto ask the clerk in the bus station, "How far can I go with this money?"

3. Why did Ernesto get so angry? Why didn't he talk to Lydia about his feelings?

4. Why did Ernesto leave town?

⟷ My Experiences

Discuss the questions with a partner.

1. Can you think of a time you told a lie or someone told you a lie? Tell the story.

2. When do you get angry?

3. Ernesto had a bad dream. Do you remember a bad dream? What happened?

 Choose one of the questions, and write about it in your journal.

Vocabulary—Working with Words

Fill in the Blanks

Complete the sentences. Use the words in the box.

clerk	confused	jealous	moved in	told a lie	woke up

1. Ernesto was tired. He went to bed early and _____ late.

2. Ernesto took all of his things to his aunt's apartment. He _____.

3. Ernesto didn't want other boys to look at Lydia. He was _____.

4. A man at the bus station sold Ernesto a ticket. He is a _____.

5. Ernesto didn't really have an American girlfriend. He _____.

6. The clerk didn't understand what Ernesto wanted. He was _____.

Vocabulary—Making the Words My Own
Vocabulary Cards

1. Choose a word you want to learn, and write it on one side of a 3 x 5 card. Write the word in big letters.

2. On the back of the card, write a sentence using that word. Then add anything that will help you remember and use this word correctly. For example, you can draw a picture, write notes about the pronunciation, give the part of speech, or write the definition.

3. When you have five or six cards, you can use them as flashcards. Look at the front and remember what's on the back. Then turn the card over to see if you were correct.

4. Put your Vocabulary Cards into groups. For example, put cards into two groups— easy words and words you need to practice more. Or put cards into three groups— nouns, verbs, and other words. Any groups are OK!

5. Work with a classmate. Use the flashcards to quiz each other.

4 **Fouad Makes a Friend**

 ## Vocabulary Preview

attacked   government   librarian   lost   safe   shout

Before We Read

1. Talk about the picture. What do you see? What is happening? What do you think will happen next?

2. Talk about the title of the chapter. What do you think Fouad wrote about?

3. Did you leave something important behind when you left your country? Talk about it.

Scanning

Read Fouad's journal entry. Answer the question.

Who is Wendy? _____

Talk about your answer with a classmate.

Fouad's Journal Entry

Read the journal entry.

Dear Group,

I am from Sudan. When soldiers attacked our village, I ran. I didn't know where. I just ran with some people. I saw my uncle Zubair. I asked him, "Where are my parents? Where are my brothers?" He shouted, "I don't know!"

We ran for many days. I lost track of time. I lost my uncle. We had no food, so we ate leaves from the trees. When we got across the border, things were better. We got food and clothes. I lived away from home for two years.

lost track of—forgot to think about

border—the official line between two countries

Then I came to the United States with help from the U.S. government. I started school in Atlanta, Georgia. I was 18 years old, so they put me in the last year of high school. I didn't have any friends. I often went to the library because I love books. Reading in English was hard at first, but I love to read. I went to the library every day after school. Sometimes I read children's books. The pictures helped me learn new words. The librarians were nice. They helped me find good books. The library was cool in the summer and warm in the winter. The library was a safe and friendly place.

When I moved to Yuma, I went to the library. Wendy, a young librarian, talked to me. She showed me pictures of her family. It was a very big family with a lot of kids. In one of the pictures I saw a man who looked familiar to me. "Who is that man?" I asked. Wendy looked at the picture carefully and said, "I'm not sure. I think he came with my cousin Facia. His name is Zu . . . Zu-something. I don't remember." I looked at the picture one more time. "Wendy!" I shouted, "I think that man is my uncle Zubair."

❓ What Happened?

Number the sentences in order.

_____ Fouad and his uncle ran away from his village.

__1__ Soldiers attacked Fouad's village.

_____ Fouad met Wendy.

_____ Fouad came to the United States.

_____ They got across the border.

_____ Fouad started school in Atlanta, Georgia.

_____ Fouad thought a man in the picture was his uncle.

_____ Fouad went to the library.

_____ They ran for many days.

_____ Wendy showed Fouad pictures of her family.

In your notebook, copy the sentences in the correct order.

Think about It

Answer the questions in a group.

1. What happened to Fouad's family?

2. Why were things better on the other side of the border?

3. Why was the library so important to Fouad?

4. Highlight or underline a sentence you like from the journal entry. Tell why you like this sentence.

⟷ My Experiences

Discuss the questions with a partner.

1. Fouad went to the library every day. Do you use the library? Why or why not?

2. What is a place you like to go to? What makes it so special?

3. Did you ever lose something important? Did you find it again?

 Choose one of the questions, and write about it in your journal.

abc Vocabulary—Working with Words

Do I Know These Words?

1. Find these words in Fouad's journal entry. Then highlight or underline them.

| attack | government | library/librarian | lose/lost | safe | shout |

2. Look at each word. Ask yourself, How well do I know this word? Write one word in each row in one of the columns.

Words	A. I don't know this word.	B. I have seen this word before.	C. I understand this word.	D. I use this word easily.
Example: party.				party
attack				
government				
library/ libraran				
Lose/lost				
safe				
shout				

3. Work in a group of three or four students. Teach your classmates the words you know. Ask them about the words you don't know well (Column A).

4. Look at your chart again. Which words can you move? Do you understand more words now?

abc Vocabulary—Making the Words My Own

Use and Remember

1. Look at the vocabulary words in earlier chapters. Which new words do you use the most? Write three of the words here.

   _____   _____   _____

2. Work with three or four classmates. Talk about your words. Explain how you will use your words in a conversation outside of class.

3. Sit with the same students during your next class. Describe when and where you used your new words. Congratulate each other on your successes!

5 Christina Makes a Change

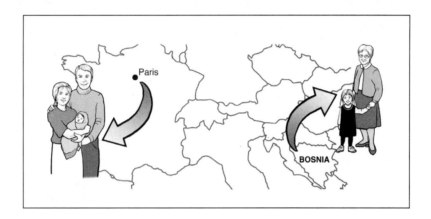

 ## Vocabulary Preview

accident   believe   find out about   glad   remember   turning point

 ## Before We Read

1. Talk about the picture. What do you see? What is happening? What do you think will happen next?

2. Talk about the title of the article. What do you think Christina wrote about?

3. Have you moved? Talk about the people, places, and things.

▷ Scanning

Read Christina's journal entry fast. Answer the questions.

Who is Michael Evans? _____

Talk about your answer with the class.

Christina's Journal Entry

Read the journal entry.

Dear Group,

I was born in Paris, but I am not French. I am Bosnian. My mother and father met in Paris. My mother worked for the Yugoslav embassy there. My father was American. My grandmother, Baba, thinks that he was a spy, but we aren't sure. I never knew my parents. They died when I was only one year old. People in Paris said my parents died in a car accident, but Baba doesn't believe them. I don't know what to believe. Baba came and took me from Paris to Bosnia. I grew up there. I don't remember anything about my mother, but I have many pictures of her, and I know a lot about her from my grandmother's stories. But I don't know anything at all about my father. I don't have any pictures of him. I only know that he was American and that his name was Michael Evans.

spy—a person who watches and listens to people secretly to get information. Spies often work for governments.

My name is Christina Evans. I like my American name. I like it when people call me "Chrissie" or "Christie." I always wanted to live in America, but I thought it was just a dream. Then, one day, when I was 18 years old, something interesting happened. Jackie Stuart, an American woman in my church, said, "Chrissie Evans, you have an American name."

"Yes, my father was American," I told her. "His name was Michael Evans."

Jackie said, "My mother's family name is Evans. My mother came from Minnesota. Was your father from Minnesota?"

Minnesota—a state in the Midwest region of the U.S.

"I don't know," I answered. "I don't know anything about my father."

This was a turning point in my life. Jackie became my friend, and she wrote a lot of letters. We wanted to find out about my father, and I wanted to go to the United States. Later the church helped me come here.

turning point—a time when things change

The people at the church here in Yuma still help me. They say, "We can find your father's family." But I don't believe them. I'm very lonely. I have no friends here, and I miss my grandmother very much. I want to stay in this country, and I want my grandmother here with me. But there are two problems. I don't have money to bring her here, and she's afraid of flying.

I write a letter to my grandmother every day. It isn't easy. I'm learning English and I'm forgetting my own language. How can that happen? I don't know.

I am glad to be in this class. I like Veronica. I like reading your journals. I like writing my journal. Maybe I can make some friends here.

❓ What Happened?

Work with a partner. Answer the questions.

1. Where was Christina born? Where did she grow up?

   _____

2. Who did Christina grow up with? Why?

   _____

3. Who helped Christina come to the United States?

   _____

4. What does Christina do every day?

   _____

5. Why can't her grandmother come to the United States?

   _____

💡 Think about It

Discuss the questions in a group.

1. Why do you think Christina likes her American name?

2. Why is it difficult for Christina to write to her grandmother?

3. Why doesn't Christina believe that she can find her father's family?

↔ My Experiences

1. How did you (or someone you know) come to the United States? In each box, draw a picture of something you remember from that trip. Then write a sentence about each picture.

1	**2**	**3**
4	**5**	**6**

_____

_____

_____

_____

_____

_____

When you finish, share your story with your classmates.

2. Make a timeline of your life. Start with the year you were born. Write important events and the dates they happened.

When you finish, explain your timeline to your partner.

3. Christina is lonely. She has no friends. But she wants to stay in the United States. Do you like living in the U.S.? Why or why not?

 Choose an event from your life. Write about it in your journal.

C Vocabulary—Working with Words

Fill in the Blanks

Complete the sentences. Use the words in the box.

accident	believe	find out about	glad	remember	turning point

1. Coming to the United States was a _____ in his life.

2. I'm _____ to see you! How have you been?

3. Do you _____ that people can live in peace?

4. After Marta's car _____, the police came to help her.

5. Eduardo has a new job. He needs to _____ the bus schedules.

6. Did Rita _____ to bring her umbrella or did she forget it?

abc Vocabulary—Making the Words My Own

Finish the Sentence

Work with a partner. Find the underlined words in the journal entry. Re-read those sentences. Then finish these sentences. Write about yourself or someone you know.

1. I don't want to have an <u>accident</u>, so _____.

2. I <u>believe</u> _____.

3. I <u>remember</u> _____.

4. I would like to <u>find out about</u> _____

   because _____.

5. _____ was a <u>turning point</u> in my life.

6. I was <u>glad</u> when _____.

6 Tadeo's Grandfather

 ## Vocabulary Preview

divide   enemy   fold   probably   protect   survived

 ## Before We Read

1. Talk about the picture. What do you see? What is happening? What do you think will happen next?

2. Talk about the title of the chapter. What do you think Tadeo wrote about?

3. Do you remember any of your grandparents? Tell what you know about them.

▷ Scanning

Read Tadeo's journal entry fast. Answer the question.

How many paper cranes did Sadako make? _____

Talk about your answer with a classmate.

Tadeo's Journal Entry

Read the journal entry.

Dear Group,

My name is Tadeo Nishimura and I am from Hiroshima, Japan.

You've probably heard about Hiroshima. The U.S. bombed this city. Maybe you heard or read the story of Sadako. Sadako was a hibakusha. A hibakusha is a person who survived the atomic attack on Hiroshima. In Hiroshima there is a statue of Sadako. She died of leukemia when she was 12 years old. When she was in the hospital, she folded 1,000 paper cranes.

After Sadako died, the crane became a symbol of peace in Japan. My grandfather was a child in Hiroshima in 1945. He was a hibakusha, too. He was very sick all his life. He wanted everyone to remember what happened. He wanted to keep atom bombs out of Japan. He wanted to keep atom bombs out of the whole world. He wanted love and peace for all people.

paper crane—a piece of colorful paper folded to look like a type of large, wild bird

symbol—a picture or shape that expresses something. For example, a shining light-bulb is a symbol of "a new idea."

Many people in Japan think Japan needs an atomic bomb to protect our country. But my grandfather and all the other hibakusha fought against this idea.

When my grandfather died, he left me all his money. He told me what I had to do with the money. I had to travel to America and meet many different people. I had to learn that all people can be friends. I had to learn that the world is not divided between friends and enemies. People may look different, and they may talk differently, but they are still the same. That's why I'm here in this class. I think my grandfather is smiling. I'm happy too!

❓ What Happened?

Mark these sentences (T) true or (F) false.

___F___ 1. Sadako is Tadeo's grandmother.

_____ 2. The United States dropped an atomic bomb on Hiroshima.

_____ 3. A hibakusha is someone who died in the atomic attack.

_____ 4. Sadako folded 2,000 paper cranes.

_____ 5. Tadeo's grandfather lived through the atomic attack.

_____ 6. His grandfather wanted Japan to build an atomic bomb.

_____ 7. Tadeo's grandfather wanted Tadeo to go to the United States.

_____ 8. His grandfather gave Tadeo all of his money.

Rewrite the false sentences, and make them true. Write them in your notebook.

Think about It

Answer the questions in a group.

1. Why do some people think that Japan needs an atomic bomb?

2. Why did Tadeo's grandfather fight against the idea of atomic bombs?

3. Why does Tadeo think his grandfather is smiling?

4. Highlight or underline a sentence you like in the journal entry. Tell your classmates why you like it.

⟷ My Experiences

Discuss the questions with a partner.

1. Tadeo's grandfather did not like atomic bombs. What do you think about atomic weapons in the world?

2. Do you think the world is divided between friends and enemies? Why or why not?

3. Tadeo wants to meet many different people. Do you have friends from other cultures? How did you meet? What is easy and what is difficult about these friendships?

 Choose one of the questions, and write about it in your journal.

Vocabulary—Working with Words

Word Families

Word families are different forms of the same word. They can help you learn a whole group of words all at one time.

Examples

I can <u>hear</u> very quiet sounds.

My grandfather doesn't have good <u>hearing</u>. I have to shout so he can <u>hear</u> me.

Have you <u>heard</u> the news?

There are people from <u>different</u> countries in our class.

I like to study <u>differently</u> from most other students.

These two cars look the same to me. I can't see any <u>difference</u> between them.

1. Here are some more word families. Write the correct form of the words in the chart.

die, died, dead, deadly, death

survive, survived, survivor, survival

protect, protected, protective, protectively, protection, protector

fold, folded, folder

Adjective	Noun	Verb	Adverb
——	hearing	hear, heard	——
different	difference	——	differently
		die, died	——
——			——
	protection		
——		fold	——

2. Write sentences. Use the words in the chart.

3. Work with a classmate. Read your sentences. Compare your sentences.

Vocabulary—Making the Words My Own

Vocabulary Challenge

Look at the preview words. How many of them can you put into one sentence? Share your sentence with the class.

Vocabulary Cards

Look again at page 15. Review your Vocabulary Cards. Make five new ones!

7 Hamad Gets an Offer

 Vocabulary Preview

admire   business   expert   garden   treasure   trip

Before We Read

1. Talk about the picture. What do you see? What is happening? What do you think will happen next?

2. Talk about the title. What do you think Hamad wrote about?

3. What flower do you like best? Why do you like it?

 Scanning

Read Hamad's journal entry fast. Answer the question.

What is *Good Gardening*? _____

Talk about your answer with a classmate.

Hamad's Journal Entry

Read the journal entry.

Dear Group,

I am a gardener from Jordan. I am probably the oldest person in this group. My name is
Hamad Al-Thani, and I am 57 years old. I am the father of two young boys, Saleh and Ali.
Saleh is 15 years old and Ali is 13. The boys' mother died five years ago. Her name was
Fatima. Fatima loved flowers, and the flower she loved best was the camellia. It is a very
unusual flower in Jordan. I grew many camellias for Fatima. When she died, I grew more and
more beautiful camellias. The flowers helped me remember her.

My two boys are my treasure. I love them and I love gardens. In Jordan I worked for the
Tadimur Landscaping Company. I always wanted my own landscaping business, but I
didn't have enough money. I had a beautiful little garden next to my house, where I grew
vegetables and Fatima's favorite flower, the camellia. I grew camellias in many colors. I
became a camellia expert. Many people came to look at my garden and admire it.

landscaping—taking care of the grass and bushes

My boss, Mr. Khalid, was a rich man. He lived outside Amman, Jordan on a lot of land. I
often worked in his garden. Sometimes I ate lunch in his kitchen. One day I found a magazine
about gardening there. It was an American magazine, *Good Gardening*. It showed many
pictures of beautiful gardens. The most beautiful one belonged to Howard Brooks in Yuma. I
loved his garden, but all of his camellias were white, not many colors like mine. Also his
camellias were short. "I think my tall camellias look better" I said out loud, "I could make his
camellias look much better."

My son, Saleh, heard me and asked, "Why don't you write to him?" Saleh knows how to
use the Internet. He could speak and write a little English. He sent an e-mail to Mr. Brooks and
included many pictures of my camellias.

Soon I got an e-mail from Mr. Brooks, "You and your boys can work in my garden," he
wrote. "Your boys can go to school here. I will pay for your trip. You and the boys can live in a
little guesthouse on my estate." I was very happy, and Saleh was happy, too. My sister,
Aisha, cried, Ali was sad, too. He said, "I don't want to go away. I don't want to leave my
friends."

guesthouse—a small house for visitors

estate—a large area of private land with a big house and other buildings

❓ What Happened?

Mark these sentences (T) true or (F) false.

___T___ 1. Hamad is a gardener.

_____ 2. Hamad has two daughters.

_____ 3. Fatima was Ali and Saleh's mother.

_____ 4. Fatima is alive.

_____ 5. Fatima loved camellias.

_____ 6. Hamad always wanted to be a doctor.

_____ 7. Hamad wrote to Mr. Brooks.

_____ 8. Mr. Brooks invited Hamad and his sons to the United States.

_____ 9. Ali wanted to go to the United States.

Rewrite the false sentences, and make them true. Write them in your notebook.

Think about It

Answer the questions in a group.

1. Why did Hamad grow more and more camellias after his wife died?

2. Why did Mr. Brooks want Hamad to work for him?

3. Do you think Hamad is lucky or unlucky? Explain your answer.

⟷ My Experiences

Discuss the questions with a partner.

1. Hamad's son Saleh helps him write an e-mail. Think about your family, neighbors, friends, and classmates. What do you do to help them? What do some of them do to help you?

2. When you were younger, did you help anyone? Who? How?

3. Hamad loves to garden. What do you like to do?

4. Hamad says, "My two boys are my treasures." What are your treasures? Why?

 Choose one of the questions, and write about it in your journal.

Vocabulary—Working With Words

Do I Know these Words?

1. Find these words in Hamad's journal entry. Then highlight or underline them.

admire	business	expert	garden	treasure	trip

2. Look at each word. Ask yourself, How well do I know this word? Write one word in each row in one of the columns (A, B, C, or D).

Words	A. I don't know this word.	B. I have seen this word before.	C. I understand this word.	D. I use this word easily.
Example: party.				party
admire				
business				
expert				
garden				
treasure				
trip				

3. Work with a group of three or four students. Teach your classmates about the words you know. Ask them about the words you don't know well.

4. Look at your chart again. Do you understand more words now? Which words can you move in your chart?

Vocabulary—Making the Words My Own

Finish the Sentence

Work with a partner. Find the underlined words in the journal entry. Re-read those sentences. Then finish these sentences. Write about yourself or someone you know.

1. My <u>treasure</u> is _____

2. In my country, one important <u>business</u> is _____

3. I am an <u>expert</u> in _____

4. I <u>admire</u> _____ because _____ .

Part 1 Checklist: How Did I Do?

Think about the things you did as you worked through Part 1. Check the things you did.

_____ I worked with a partner or a group.

_____ I asked questions when I didn't understand something.

_____ I wrote journal entries.

_____ I made vocabulary cards.

_____ I added words to my vocabulary house.

_____ I used new vocabulary in and out of class.

_____ I read the stories once without using my dictionary.

_____ I highlighted or underlined important words or sentences in the journals.

_____ I reviewed what we studied in class when I went home.

What things do you want to try that you didn't do? Write one or two things that you will try in the next unit.

_____

_____

Share your answers with two or three classmates.

Veronica's Second Letter

 ## Scanning

Read Veronica's letter fast. Answer the question.

Why is Veronica happy for Fouad? _____

Talk about your answer with a classmate.

Veronica's Letter

Read the letter.

Dear Students,

I always enjoy reading your journals. All of your stories are fascinating. I read one journal and say to myself, "What a good story." Then I read the next one and again I say, "Wow! Another good story." Last week I told some of your stories to my husband, and he said, "Wow! What wonderful stories. I'd like to meet your students some time."

Lydia, I felt like I was sitting with you at that mailbox, and I was glad when Ernesto and Fouad became friends. I was also very happy that Fouad found the library. I love libraries, too. Christina, I am pleased that you like your American name. Not everyone likes the American form of their name. Tadeo, I am so happy that your grandfather sent you to us, and Hamad, what a good thing that your son could use the Internet and help you and Howard Brooks find each other.

I told my husband that we all really do have wonderful stories. Sometimes we just forget to tell our stories, and sometimes we don't listen carefully enough to the stories that other people tell us.

Let's keep on telling our stories and listening carefully to each other.
Veronica

 ## Think about It

What do you think will happen in Part 2?

8 Ernesto Changes His Life

 ## abc Vocabulary Preview

clean   forgive   invite   lonely   right away   spoil

Before We Read

1. Talk about the picture. What do you see? What is happening? What do you think will happen next?

2. Talk about the title of the chapter. What do you think Lydia wrote about?

3. Is anger sometimes bad? Sometimes good? Explain and give examples.

Scanning

Read Ernesto's journal entry fast. Answer the question.

Where do Adriana and Lydia work? _____

Talk about your answer with a partner.

Ernesto's Journal Entry

Read the journal entry.

Dear Group,

I am romantic. There is only one true love in my life. Lydia is my true love. My sister Adriana sent me an e-mail. She told me, "Lydia is sad. She misses you. She has no other boyfriend." I was angry. I didn't believe her.

romantic—showing feelings of love

Then Adriana called me on the phone. "Ernesto, don't be stupid!" she said. "Lydia loves you. She wants to see you. She wants to see you very much." I was still angry, but Fouad, my roommate, agreed with Adriana. "Ernesto" he said. "Your anger is spoiling your life." I didn't believe any of them. But then a letter came from Lydia—a beautiful letter. She still loved me. She didn't care about those other boys.

I called Lydia right away. "I love you, Lydia." I said. "I lied because I wanted to make you jealous. I don't have an American girlfriend. I'm very sorry. You are my only love. Can you forgive me?" We talked and talked. Lydia cried a lot.

That telephone call changed my life. Soon Lydia and Adriana moved to Yuma. They live with my Aunt Teresa now. They both work in a beauty salon, and they study at a beauty school. They're also students in this English class. Lydia and Adriana like living with my Aunt Teresa, and she likes it, too. She says, "I was lonely before the girls came. I am happier now." There are two bedrooms in Aunt Teresa's apartment. The girls rent one of the bedrooms. They say, "Aunt Teresa is like a second mother to us."

beauty salon—a place where people get fashionable haircuts, manicures, etc.

Fouad and I like to visit the girls. Aunt Teresa's apartment is always nice and clean, and she's a wonderful cook. On Saturdays she and the girls bake. Good smells come from that kitchen. They always invite Fouad and me for Saturday dinner. The food is good, and their house feels like home to me. But the best part of Aunt Teresa's apartment is that Lydia lives there.

❓ What Happened?

Mark these sentences (T) true or (F) false.

    _F_   1. Adriana wrote a letter to her brother.

    _____ 2. Fouad was angry.

    _____ 3. Ernesto lied to Lydia.

    _____ 4. Fouad told Ernesto not to be angry.

    _____ 5. Aunt Teresa was lonely before the girls came.

    _____ 6. Teresa is Lydia's aunt.

    _____ 7. Adriana is Ernesto's sister.

    _____ 8. Aunt Teresa doesn't like to cook.

Rewrite the false sentences, and make them true. Write them in your notebook.

Think about It

Answer the questions in a group.

1. Why did Lydia cry when Ernesto called her?

2. How did the telephone call change Ernesto's life?

3. Ernesto thinks he is romantic. Do you agree? Explain your answer.

4. The girls say that Aunt Teresa is like a second mother to them. What does this mean?

5. What might happen next?

↔ My Experiences

Discuss the questions with a partner.

1. Ernesto's phone call to Lydia changed his life. Can you think of something that changed your life? Tell the story.

2. Who is the most important person in your life, other than your parents? Explain your answer.

3. What is one happy memory from your childhood?

4. Do people have only one true love in their lives? Explain.

 Choose one of the questions, and write about it in your journal.

Vocabulary—Working with Words

Fill in the Blanks

Complete the sentences. Use the words in the box.

clean	forgive	invite	lonely	right away	spoil

1. Celia's friends forgot her birthday. She was angry, but she decided to _____ them. Now she feels better, and her friends do too.

2. If Lydia leaves Ernesto, it will _____ Ernesto's life.

3. Mehmet's bicycle is broken. He needs to fix it _____ so he can get to work.

4. I'm having a birthday party. I want to _____ all my friends.

5. My house is dirty. I need to _____ it before the party.

6. Sharon was _____ when she first came to the United States, but now she has a lot of friends.

abc Vocabulary—Making the Words My Own

Use and Remember

1. Look at the vocabulary words in earlier chapters. Which new words are the most important for you? Write three of the words here.

   _____   _____   _____

2. Work with three or four classmates. Talk about your words. Explain how you will use your words in a conversation outside of class.

3. Sit with the same students during your next class. Describe when and where you used your new words. Congratulate each other on your success.

9 Lydia Moves Out

Vocabulary Preview

definitely   follow her heart   insisted   leave home   make plans   take care of

Before We Read

1. Talk about the picture. What do you see? What is happening? What do you think will happen next?

2. Talk about the title of the chapter. What do you think Lydia wrote about?

3. What do you remember about Lydia? Who is her boyfriend? Who is her best friend? What else do you remember about her?

4. Did you ever disagree with your parents? What happened?

Scanning

Read Lydia's journal entry fast. Answer the question.

Who is Angelica? _____

Talk about your answer with a classmate.

Lydia's Journal Entry

Read the journal entry.

Dear Group,

I cried many nights. I couldn't sleep. I missed Ernesto. I was working in a department store, but I didn't like my job. Miss Ellis was my boss. She said, "You need to speak English better. And you need to dress better and smile more. You have to be friendly." But I didn't know the right words, I didn't feel pretty, and I definitely didn't feel friendly.

Things weren't going well at home, either. My mom was always angry. She missed her friends and her sisters in Mexico. She needed my help. She was always saying, "Do the dishes, Lydia!" "Change the baby's diaper, Lydia!" "Clear the table, Lydia!" "Take the coffee to your father, Lydia."

> **diaper**—cloth that a baby wears before he or she can use a toilet

"Hang out the clothes, Lydia!"

Ernesto's sister Adriana is my best friend. She worked in a beauty shop. Adriana said, "Ernesto loves you." But I didn't believe her. One day Ernesto called me. He got my letter, and he needed to talk. He said, "I love you, Lydia. There is no American girlfriend. There is only you. There was always only you."

He was still my Ernesto! Everything changed. My heart bloomed, and I felt like I was the real Lydia again. I wanted to go to Yuma to be near Ernesto.

Adriana and I made plans. A few days later, Adriana's parents came to talk with my mother and father. Adriana's father said, "Lydia and Adriana want to move to Yuma. They can live with my sister, Teresa. She will enjoy the girls, and she can take good care of them."

Then Adriana's mother said, "There is a good beauty school in Yuma. The girls can study there." And her father added, "Yuma has a good English-language school."

But my mother was sad. "Lydia is my oldest daughter," she said. "I need her help. And she is still too young to leave home." My father said, "Hmmmm . . . hmmm . . . "

"A daughter stays home to help her mother," my mother insisted. My father said, "Hmmm . . . hmmmm." "I will miss Lydia very much," my mother said, more softly.

My father was very quiet. He looked at me for a long time. Then he put his arm around my mother. "Angelica," he said very quietly. "We live in The United States now. Life here is very different. Our Lydia is a young woman. She must find her own life here. She must follow her heart."

Two weeks later my parents drove Adriana and me to Yuma. We love living with Aunt Teresa. Adriana and I are learning a lot of English. There is just one bad thing. There is a student in the beauty school, Scott Andrews. He wants to be a barber. I don't like the way he looks at me, and I don't like the way he talks to me.

❓ What Happened?

Work with a partner. Answer the questions.

1. Lydia _____ sleep because she missed Ernesto.

   a. couldn't   b. could

2. Lydia's boss said she needed to dress better and _____ more.

   a. smile   b. eat

3. She was _____ at home.

   a. happy   b. unhappy

4. She _____ pretty.

   a. didn't feel   b. felt

5. Angelica is _____.

   a. Lydia's mother   b. Ernesto's mother

6. Lydia went to Yuma to _____.

   a. be near Ernesto   b. help her mother

7. Lydia and Adriana live with _____.

   a. Adriana's mother   b. Adriana's aunt

 # Think about It

Answer the questions in a group.

1. Lydia didn't feel pretty or friendly. Can you explain why?

2. Lydia's mother and father have very different ideas about their daughter's plans. Can you explain why?

3. Highlight or underline a sentence you like in the journal entry. Tell your classmates why you like it.

↔ My Experiences

Discuss the questions with a partner.

1. Sometimes immigrant parents and their children disagree. What things do they usually disagree about? Why do you think this happens?

2. What is something you disagreed about with a family member?

 Choose one of the questions, and write about it in your journal.

abc Vocabulary—Working with Words

Fill in the Blanks

definitely	insisted	follow her heart	leave home	make plans	take care of

1. Lydia left home to be with Ernesto, and _____.

2. My mother wanted me to get good grades. "Study hard," she _____.

3. Adriana's aunt will _____ the girls. They will live with her, and she will help them.

4. Marco didn't do well on his test. He will _____ study harder next time.

5. Lydia's mother was sad that Lydia wanted to _____.

6. Let's _____ for tonight. Do you want to go to a movie?

abc Vocabulary—Making the Words My Own

Vocabulary Cards

Look at page 15, and review your vocabulary cards. Keep making new ones! Choose more words you want to learn, and write them on 3 x 5 cards. Play Categories by putting your cards into groups. Explain your groups to a partner.

10 Fouad Feels Lucky

Vocabulary Preview

explain   prefer   sour   sweet   touch   unlucky

Before We Read

1. Talk about the picture. What do you see? What is happening? What do you think will happen next?

2. Talk about the title of the chapter. What do you think Fouad wrote about?

3. What do you remember about Fouad?

4. Where do you like to go with friends? What do you do there? Work with a group of three or four students, and tell your story.

Scanning

Read Fouad's journal entry fast. Answer the question.

Who likes a doughnut with her coffee? _____

Talk about your answer with a classmate.

Fouad's Journal Entry

Read the journal entry.

Dear Group,

Yesterday Wendy and I went out for coffee. I took Wendy to my favorite coffee shop. I love to go there. Many people sit at round tables and talk. Some students do their schoolwork. Others work on their laptops. Sometimes a young man plays his guitar, and people sing when he plays a song that they know. The coffee smells and tastes wonderful. They serve coffee in big white cups. There are flower boxes in the windows. There are magazines and newspapers here and there. I love being in this coffee shop.

Wendy likes her coffee strong and black. She likes a doughnut with her coffee. I like my coffee with lots of milk but no sugar. I like a sandwich with my coffee. I don't like sweet things. I prefer sour things like pickles on my turkey sandwich. I like lots of mustard on my turkey sandwich, too.

Wendy said, "I love this place. I'm glad we came here." I said, "Me, too. I feel very lucky to be here with you." Wendy thought for a moment, "I'm glad you feel lucky," she said, "because sometimes when I think about you and how you lost your family, I feel very angry. I wonder why things happen the way they do. Sometimes good things happen to bad people, and bad things happen to good people. How can you explain that?"

I said, "We can't explain everything, Wendy. But I know one thing. We all need friends. Maybe I was unlucky to lose my family. But I found friends, and that makes me feel lucky."

"You're right. We all need friends to be happy," Wendy said. "I'm glad you and I are friends." And she touched my hand.

❓ What Happened?

Work with a partner. Answer the questions.

1. What do people do in a coffee shop?

   _____

2. What does Wendy eat and drink there?

   _____

3. What foods does Fouad like?

   _____

4. What did Wendy do at the end?

   _____

Copy your answers in your notebook.

Think about It

Answer the questions in a group.

1. Why do Fouad and Wendy like the coffee shop?

2. Why does Wendy feel angry? Why does Fouad feel lucky?

3. How do Wendy and Fouad feel about each other?

4. Highlight or underline a sentence you like from the journal entry. Tell your classmates why you like this sentence.

↔ My Experiences

Discuss the questions with a partner.

1. Do you have a favorite coffee shop or restaurant? Talk about what it looks like and why do you like it.

2. What are you grateful for in your life? Why?

3. At the end of Fouad's journal entry, Wendy touches Fouad's hand. Does this touch mean something special?

4. In the United States, some people are comfortable touching in public. When is it OK to touch in your culture?

 Choose one of the questions, and write about it in your journal.

Vocabulary—Working with Words

Fill in the Blanks

Complete the sentences. Use the words in the box.

explain	prefer	sour	sweet	touch	unlucky

1. I don't understand this grammar. Can you _____ it to me?

2. Her sister loves _____ foods. She can eat a lemon!

3. I don't like chocolate. It's too _____ for me.

4. Javier lost a $20 bill! He's _____ today.

5. Do you _____ coffee or tea?

6. Don't _____ that! It's really hot!

abc Vocabulary—Making the Words My Own

Categories

Work together with a group, and list these words in the following categories according to their strongest flavor. (Some foods might have a combination of flavors. Choose the one you think is strongest.)

cake	ham	miso soup
candy	ice cream	soy sauce
cookies	lemons	strong coffee
grapefruit	lemon rind (the skin of a lemon)	very dark chocolate
green apples	limes	vinegar

sweet	salty	sour	bitter

Add more foods that you know to each group.

a. Bring in different foods that you like to share with your classmates. Discuss the flavor.

b. Internet search: Find out more about flavors. Look up a 5th flavor—umami.

Tell your classmates how often you eat the foods in your chart. Every week? Sometimes? Never? Are there foods you would like to try?

abc Mid-Part Vocabulary Review

Look back at the words you are learning from earlier chapters. Alone, in pairs, or in groups, review these words. You might use Vocabulary Cards (page 15), Vocabulary House (page 10), or Vocabulary Challenge (page 31) to do this.

11 Christina Gets a Surprise

 ## Vocabulary Preview

busy   customers   package   proud of   tips   worried (about)

 ## Before We Read

1. Talk about the picture. What do you see? What is happening? What do you think will happen next?

2. Talk about the title of the chapter. What do you think Christina wrote about?

3. What do you remember about Christina's story? Who is Jackie Stuart?

4. Do you have a job? What do you do? Do you like it? Explain your answer.

▷ Scanning

Read Christina's journal entry fast. Answer the question.

What happened to the shoe factory? _____

Talk about your answer with a classmate.

Christina's Journal Entry

Read the journal entry.

Dear Group,

I have good news. I found a job in a restaurant. I'm a server. I really like the job. I like talking with the customers, and I like bringing them good food. Most people are happy when they eat out. Some leave big tips. On Friday Mrs. Manning, the owner of the restaurant, talked to me. She said, "You're doing a very good job, Chrissie. I'm happy with your work." I felt proud. I'm doing well in my first American job.

Last week I got two interesting letters. The first one was from Baba. I'm worried about her. She misses me, and she is not well. Our neighbors help her with food, but it isn't easy. The factory in our village closed. Farming is also difficult because there are land mines all over the countryside. My grandmother wants to come to the United States to live with me, but she's afraid of flying. I would have to go there and fly back with her. I hope to save enough money from my job at the restaurant to get plane tickets for both of us. Baba also sent me a package of my favorite sweet—her homemade baklava.

land mines—bombs in the ground that explode when someone touches them.

I also got a surprising letter! It was in English. It was from a woman in Minnesota. Her name is Ruth Evans. This is what she wrote:

> Dear Christina,
>
> My name is Ruth Evans. I own a dress shop in Minneapolis, Minnesota. I am 63 years old. I am a mother and a grandmother. I had two sons, but now I have only one.
>
> His name is Matthew. For many years I thought this was my whole family, but I recently got a letter from my cousin Jackie Stuart. She met you in Bosnia. She told me about you, and she sent me a picture of you.
>
> I think that you and I might be related to each other. May I come to Yuma and meet you? I know you are very busy. Can you meet me sometime on Saturday or Sunday? Please call and tell me when and where we can meet. I want to talk with you and show you some family pictures.
>
> My telephone number is 626-555-9683.
>
> Sincerely,
>
> Ruth Evans

Well, dear writing friends, what do you think about that? I called Ruth right away. I was so excited that I forgot all my English. I started to talk to Ruth in Bosnian. Ruth just laughed. She seems very nice. I am going to meet her this Sunday.

? What Happened?

Complete the sentences. Then discuss them with your classmates. Are you answers different or the same?

1. Christina likes her new job because _____.

2. Christina feels proud because _____.

3. Christina received two letters. The first letter was from _____. The second letter was from _____.

4. Christina's grandmother in Bosnia wants to _____.

5. Ruth Evans wants to _____.

 # Think about It

Answer the questions in a group.

1. Is Christina a good server? Explain your answer.

2. Is her grandmother happy in Bosnia? Why or why not?

3. Why does Christina start to speak Bosnian to Ruth Evans?

4. Do you think Christina is related to Ruth Evans? If so, how do you think they might be related?

5. What might happen next?

←→ My Experiences

Discuss the questions with your class.

1. Christina is proud of doing well in her first American job. What are you proud of?

   Complete this sentence *I'm proud of* _____

Walk around, and talk to your classmates about their sentences, complete the chart.

Name	is proud of . . .

2. What was your first job? Did you like it? How did you find it?

 Choose one of the questions, and write about it in your journal.

abc Vocabulary—Working with Words
Categories

1. Read the words. They are all words that describe feelings.

   angry, sorry, afraid, stupid, ashamed, hungry, tired, thirsty, sad

   jealous, safe, glad, happy, lucky

   proud, surprised, worried, afraid, excited

2. Write about the people in Veronica's class. For example,

   When other boys looked at Lydia, Ernesto was _____

3. Read your sentences to a partner.

4. Write the words that describe feelings in the chart. (It's OK if you and your classmates put the words in different places.)

Good Feelings	Bad Feelings	Feelings Good or Bad

Take turns telling your classmates about times when you had some of these feelings.

Vocabulary—Working with Words

Fill in the Blanks

Complete the sentences. Use the words in the box.

busy	customers	package	proud of	tips	worried (about)

1. When you eat at a restaurant, you should leave the server a _____.

2. I can't talk to you now. I'm very _____. I'm making dinner.

3. People who spend money in a store or a restaurant are _____.

4. Sophia got an A on her English test. She felt _____ herself.

5. Ivan's father sent him a big _____ from Bosnia.

6. We'll help you repair your car. You don't have to be _____ it.

Vocabulary—Making the Words My Own

Finish the Sentence

Work with a partner. Find the underlined words in the journal entry. Re-read those sentences. Then finish these sentences. Write about yourself or someone you know.

1. Customers come to a store to _____.

2. Usually customers give tips to _____.

3. I felt proud of _____.

4. Don't worry about _____.

5. When I opened the package, I found _____.

6. I'm too busy to _____.

12 Tadeo Volunteers

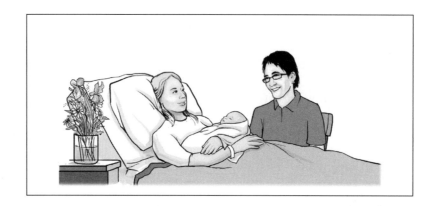

 ## Vocabulary Preview

during   nurse   patients   sadness   visitor   volunteer

 ## Before We Read

1. Talk about the picture. What do you see? What is happening?

2. Talk about the title of the chapter. What do you think Tadeo wrote about?

3. What do you remember about Tadeo?

4. What is volunteering? What are some things people volunteer to do? Why do you think people volunteer?

▷ Scanning

Read Tadeo's journal entry fast. Answer the question.

Who is Eric? _____

Talk about your answer with a classmate.

Tadeo's Journal Entry

Read the journal entry.

Dear Group,

I just read Christina's journal, and I am happy for her. Maybe she has an American family, but she also has to think about her grandmother in Bosnia. I'm curious about how she can travel back to Bosnia and bring her grandmother to the United States. Maybe our class can help her. What do you think?

I had an interesting month. This class is good, and the writing journals are good, but sometimes I feel lonely. I don't want to go back to Japan, but I feel alone here. It's hard for me to get up in the morning. Sometimes I'm sad for no reason. Anyway, no reason I can think of. Last week I decided to do something about my sadness.

Veronica told us that many Americans do volunteer work. I decided to volunteer at Yuma General Hospital. It's a good way to meet people. I thought if I helped other people I might feel better myself. It's also a good way to learn English. Now I volunteer at the hospital for five hours at night, three times a week.

I help patients get to the bathroom safely. I help visitors find patients, and sometimes I just talk with the patients. They tell me about their health problems and about their families. Some of them have no family. Some of them want to learn about life in Japan, and I'm happy to tell them. One patient, Mrs. Rogers, said, "Japan sounds wonderful, Tadeo. I hope to go there. Maybe I can meet your family."

I like the maternity ward best. It's always full of flowers, and the babies are beautiful. The new mothers look proud and happy. I bring them books and newspapers.

maternity ward— the section of the hospital where women have babies

I met Eric in the hospital. He is a nurse. He works very hard both during the day and sometimes at night. He works in surgery, but he visits the patients after surgery.

surgery—the department in a hospital that does operations on patients

Eric is a single father. His daughter, Carol, is 13 years old. Carol, Eric, and I often eat together in the hospital cafeteria. I enjoy their company.

enjoy their company—like being with them

? What Happened?

Work with a partner. Answer the questions.

1. Why is Tadeo happy for Christina?

   _____

2. Why is it hard for Tadeo to get up in the morning?

   _____

3. What did he decide to do to feel better?

   _____

4. What are some things he does in the hospital?

   _____

5. How often he does volunteer at the hospital?

   _____

6. Why does he like the maternity ward?

   _____

7. What do we know about Eric?

   _____

 # Think about It

Answer the questions in a group.

1. Why doesn't Tadeo want to go back to Japan?

2. Why does he like working in the hospital? Give as many reasons as you can.

3. Why does Tadeo enjoy spending time with Eric and Carol?

4. What might happen next?

⟷ My Experiences

Discuss the questions with your class.

1. Tadeo volunteers in a hospital. How are hospitals or doctor's offices in the U.S. different from hospitals or doctor's offices in other places?

2. Would you like to do volunteer work? What would you like to do? Explain your answer.

3. Tadeo volunteers because he wants to feel better. What do you do to feel better?

 Choose one of the questions and write about it in your journal.

Vocabulary—Working with Words

Word Families

You learned some word families in Chapter 6. Word Families help you learn a whole group of words at one time.

1. Here are some more word families. Write the correct form of the words in the chart.

   sad, sadness

   lonely

   proudly, volunteer, volunteers,

   hopefully, hopeful, hope

   safely. safety

Adjective	Noun	Verb	Adverb
		————	sadly
	loneliness	———	———
proud	.	———	
	volunteer	———	voluntarily
		hope	
safe		———	

2. Write sentences, use the words in the chart.

3. Work with a class mate. Read your sentences and listen to their sentences. Compare them.

Vocabulary—Making the Words My Own

Vocabulary House

1. Look again at page 10. Take out your Vocabulary House. In small groups, talk about the words in each room. Tell why you put those words there.

2. Choose new words you want to remember. Decide where to write them in your Vocabulary House, and tell your group why.

Vocabulary Challenge

Look at the six words in Vocabulary Preview. How many of them can you use in one sentence? Share your sentence with the class.

13 Hamad Sees the School Principal

 ## Vocabulary Preview

gifted   lazy   principal   (in a state of) shock   smart   special

Before We Read

1. Talk about the picture. What do you see? What is happening?

2. Talk about the title of the chapter. What do you think will happen?

3. What do you remember about Hamad?

4. What is a good student?

5. How are schools in the U.S. different from schools in another country?

Scanning

Read Hamad's journal entry fast. Answer the question.

Who is Mrs. Adams? _____

Talk about your answers with a classmate.

Hamad's Journal Entry

Read the journal entry.

Dear Group,

I had a very strange week. I have a problem. It is a good problem, I think, but it is still a problem. My son Ali is too smart for his American school. In Jordan Ali was never smart in school. The teachers always said, "Ali is lazy. He doesn't listen."

Last week Ali's American teacher, Dwight Fitzroy, asked me to come to school. I thought he would say, "Ali is lazy. Ali doesn't listen." But Mr. Fitzroy didn't say those things. Instead he said, "Mr. Al-Thani, your son Ali is a gifted child. He learned English fast. He also understands a lot of math. He learns everything I teach, and then he goes to the computer and learns more all by himself.

He already knows U.S. history and world geography. And he knows more about botany than I do! Ali needs to go to a special school for gifted children. He needs special teachers."

"I am still new here in the United States. I don't know anything about special schools." I told Mr. Fitzroy. Mr. Fitzroy said, "I will help you, and Mrs. Adams, our principal, will help you too." Then we went to Mrs. Adams' office.

Mrs. Adams said, "Please sit down, Mr. Al-Thani. Do you want some coffee?" I said, "Yes, please." I drank the coffee. It was terrible American coffee, but I didn't care. I was in a state of shock. It was happy shock. Mrs. Adams talked a lot. I didn't understand everything, but I do understand that Ali needs a new school. I am going to talk to Howard about this. You probably remember that Howard Brooks is my employer. Now he is also my good friend. I like to talk things over with him.

When I told Ali all of this, he was happy. "I like school in the United States." he said.

What Happened?

Mark the sentences (T) true or (F) false.

_____ 1. Hamad has a problem.

_____ 2. Ali is lazy.

_____ 3. Ali learned English fast.

_____ 4. Ali doesn't like computers.

_____ 5. Mr. Fitzroy wants Ali to go to a special school.

_____ 6. Ali doesn't like school in the United States.

Rewrite the false sentences and make them true. Write them in your notebook.

Think about It

Answer the questions in a group.

1. Why was Hamad surprised?

2. Why did Ali's teachers in Jordan think he was lazy?

3. Why does Mr. Fitzroy think Ali is gifted?

4. Why does Ali like his U.S. school?

5. What might happen next?

⟷ My Experiences

Discuss these questions with your class.

1. How do you like to learn?

   _____ I like to listen to my teacher.

   _____ I like to listen to something many times.

   _____ I like to try things myself.

   _____ I like to watch someone do something.

   _____ I like to work with someone who knows more than I do.

   _____ I like to read.

   _____ I like to write things down.

   _____ I like to pay attention in class.

Complete the sentence:

   I like to _____.

Walk around the class. Talk to your classmates about their sentences. Complete the chart.

Name	likes to . . .

Tell the class something you learned about a classmate.

2. Ali's teachers in Jordan said he was a lazy student. His teachers in the United States think he is gifted. What kind of student were you when you were young? What kind of student are you now?

 Choose one of the questions, and write about it in your journal.

abc Vocabulary—Working with Words

Fill in the Blanks

Complete the sentences. Use the words in the box.

gifted	lazy	principal	in a state of shock	smart	special

1. Ming can paint beautiful pictures, and he plays the guitar, too. Everyone says he is
   _____.

2. My mother always makes a _____ chocolate cake for my birthday.

3. Alex works all day. Then he goes home and helps his wife. He is definitely not
   _____.

4. The head of our school is the _____.

5. Pamela gets good grades in school. Her teachers say she's very _____.

6. My uncle was in an accident, and he couldn't remember anything. The doctors said he
   was _____.

abc Vocabulary—Making the Words My Own

Use and Remember

1. Look at the vocabulary words in earlier chapters. Which new words are the most
   important for you? Write three of the words here.

   _____   _____   _____

2. Work with three or four classmates. Talk about your words. Explain how you will use
   your words in a conversation outside of class.

3. Sit with the same students during your next class. Describe when and where you used
   your new words. Congratulate each other on your successes.

Part 2 Checklist: How Did I Do?

Think about the things you did as you worked through Part 2.
Check the things you did.

_____ I worked with a partner or a group in class.

_____ I asked questions when I didn't understand something.

_____ I wrote a journal.

_____ I made vocabulary cards.

_____ I added words to my Vocabulary House.

_____ I used new vocabulary in and out of class.

_____ I read the stories once without using my dictionary.

_____ I used a highlighter to highlight important words or sentences in the journals.

_____ I reviewed what we studied in class after I went home.

What things do you want to try that you didn't do? Write one or two ideas that you
will try in the next unit.

_____

_____

Share your answers with two or three classmates.

PART 3

Twists and Turns

Veronica's Third Letter

 ## Scanning

Read Veronicas' letter fast. Answer the question.

Where is Veronica moving? _____

Talk about your answer with a classmate.

Veronica's Letter

Read the letter.

Dear Students,

I gave everyone in class a copy of Christina's journal entries and also Tadeo's suggestion that we might help Christina bring her grandmother from Bosnia to the United States. I suggest a bake sale. I really like to bake, and I have a big kitchen.

You are welcome to come to my house. We can bake cakes and cookies in my kitchen. I have a big oven. I have many baking pans. I have a lot of flour, butter, and sugar. I have many good recipes for cakes, pies, and cookies. It will be fun to bake together. We can sell our cakes, pies, and cookies to the whole school. We can use the money to help Christina bring her grandmother to the United States. What do you think?

I also want to tell you that I am leaving Yuma at the end of this school year. I'm moving to Tucson because my husband found a job there. You are my last class in Yuma. I am nervous about moving to a new city. Because all of you are new here in Yuma, maybe you can give me some advice.

Veronica

 ## Think about It

What do you think will happen in Part 3?

14 Lydia Has a Problem

 Vocabulary Preview

delicious   delighted   disappear   funny   suggestion   uncomfortable

 Before We Read

Look again at Veronica's letter.

1. What was Tadeo's suggestion? What did Veronica suggest? Do you think this is a good idea? Why or why not?

2. Talk about the picture. What do you see? What do you think will happen next?

3. Talk about the title of the chapter. What do you think Lydia wrote about?

4. What do you remember about Lydia?

▷ **Scanning**

Read Lydia's journal entry fast. Answer the question.

What is Ernesto going to buy for his aunt? _____

Talk about your answer with a classmate.

Lydia's Journal Entry

Read the journal entry.

Dear Group,

I like Veronica's suggestion about having a bake sale. We can use Aunt Teresa's kitchen, too. Aunt Teresa can make wonderful Mexican cakes. She makes delicious pumpkin tamales and capirotada. Capirotada is a bread pudding. It tastes wonderful!

Yesterday I asked Aunt Teresa, "Can our class bake in your kitchen? We want to help Christina bring her grandmother to the United States from Bosnia."

Aunt Teresa was delighted. "What a wonderful idea!" She said, "I want to help too!"

Last Saturday Fouad and Ernesto came to dinner. Adriana and I helped Aunt Teresa make a delicious meal. They did the dishes. Ernesto said, "You need a dishwasher. I'm going to buy you one!"

I am learning a lot at beauty school. In the beginning, I could only shampoo people. Now I also do haircuts, and I'm learning how to color hair. I like talking to the customers. They tell me about their lives, and they ask me about my life. Yesterday a woman came to get a new hair color. She wanted to look nice for her daughter's wedding. I made her look beautiful. She loved her new look. I felt very proud.

shampoo—wash hair

wedding—a ceremony between two people to be married

Someday Adriana and I want to have our own beauty salon. I really like beauty school, but Scott Andrews still makes me feel uncomfortable. I don't like the jokes he makes. I try to laugh at his jokes, but I really don't think they are funny. When he looks at me, I want to disappear.

What Happened?

Work with a partner. Answer the questions.

1. How did Fouad and Ernesto help? _____

2. What does Ernesto want to buy for Aunt Teresa? _____

3. What is Lydia learning? _____

4. Why did Lydia feel proud? _____

5. Who makes Lydia feel uncomfortable? _____

Think about It

Discuss the questions in a group.

1. Why is Aunt Teresa delighted?

2. Do you think Lydia and Adriana will have their own beauty salon someday? Explain your answer.

3. Why does Scott Andrews make Lydia feel uncomfortable?

4. What might happen next?

↔ My Experiences

Discuss the questions with a partner.

1. Lydia goes to ESL classes and also to beauty school. What are you learning at school? What do you like about school?

2. What kind of work do you do? What kind of work do you want to do in the future?

3. Do you think men and women are equal? Explain your answer.

4. Do you think men's and women's roles are changing? If so, how?

 Choose one of the questions and write about it in your journal.

abc Vocabulary—Working with Words

Do I Know These Words?

1. Find these words in Lydia's journal entry. Then highlight or underline them.

| delicious | delighted | disappear | funny | suggestion | uncomfortable |

2. Look at each word. Ask yourself, How well do I know this word? Write one word in each row in one of the columns (A, B, C, or D).

Words	A. I don't know this word.	B. I have seen this word before.	C. I understand this word.	D. I use this word easily.
Example: party.				party
delicious				
delighted				
disappear				
funny				
suggestion				
uncomfortable				

3. Work with a group of three or four students. Teach your classmates about the words you know. Ask them about the words you don't know well.

4. Look at your chart again. Do you understand more words now? Which words can you move in your chart?

Vocabulary—Making the Words My Own

Finish the Sentence

Work with a partner. Find the underlined words in the journal entry. Re-read those sentences. Then finish these sentences. Write about yourself or someone you know.

1. I feel <u>uncomfortable</u> when _____.

2. I have a <u>suggestion</u>! Let's _____.

3. My smile <u>disappeared</u> when _____.

4. _____ cooks <u>delicious</u> food.

5. I was <u>delighted</u> when _____.

6. I saw something really <u>funny</u>! It was _____.

Vocabulary Cards

Look again at page 15. Review your Vocabulary Cards. Make five new ones!

15 Ernesto Gets Angry

 ## Vocabulary Preview

beat someone up   leak   repair   satisfied   taste   upset

Before We Read

1. Talk about the picture. What do you see? What is happening?

2. Talk about the title of the chapter. What do you think Ernesto wrote about?

3. What do you remember about Ernesto?

4. Describe something you do well.

 ## Scanning

Read Ernesto's journal entry fast. Answer the question.

What is Ernesto's big news? _____

Talk about your answer with a classmate.

Ernesto's Journal Entry

Read the journal entry.

Dear Group,

Yesterday some of us baked at Aunt Teresa's house. It was the first time I tried to bake. My mother never allowed me in the kitchen, but today I made brownies. The people who tasted them said they were good. Lydia made an apple pie, and Adriana made a chocolate cake. I liked Tadeo's banana bread the best.

My big news is that I have a new job. I work in a garage. I'm good with cars. I really enjoy the work. I can strip your carburetor, repair your gearshift, or fix a leak in your air-conditioning system. I can check your tire pressure, change your engine oil, and even repair your steering system. I make cars safer to drive. Jerry Breck and his son David own the garage. They're friendly, and they work hard. They pay me well and they are satisfied with my work. Mr. Breck says, "You have golden hands, Ernesto." That makes me feel a little embarrassed, but I also feel proud.

I do have one problem. Scott Andrews, a barber in Lydia's school, says bad things to Lydia. It upsets her very much. Lydia says it will be OK, but I don't think so. This guy makes me very angry. I want to beat him up. What can I do?

❓ What Happened?

Work with a partner. Answer the questions.

1. Why didn't Ernesto learn to cook when he was a child? _____

2. What does Ernesto do at his new job? _____

3. Why does Ernesto like his job? _____

4. How does Ernesto feel about Scott Andrews? Why? _____

Think about It

Answer the questions with your group.

1. What is changing for Ernesto? Why?

2. Lydia says about Scott Andrews, "It will be OK." Ernesto doesn't agree. Why do you think that is true?

3. Why didn't Ernesto's mother let him in the kitchen when he was a boy?

4. What might happen next?

⟷ My Experiences

Discuss the questions with a partner.

1. Ernesto has a new job. Tell about a job you like or liked. The job can be at home or outside of the house. What did you like about it? What were you good at?

2. What do you expect from a job outside of home? Read the chart. Then number the job features from 1 (the most important to you) to 10 (the least important to you).

My numbers	Job feature
	New friends
	Good people to work with
	Interesting work
	Creative work
	Advancement
	Good boss
	Good salary
	Good benefits
	Pleasant workplace
	other_____

Work with three or four classmates to explain your answers.

 Choose one of your questions, and write about it in your journal.

abc Vocabulary—Working with Words

Categories

Read the words in the box.

angry	engine	leak	repair
bad	enjoy	pay	satisfied
bake	fix	proud	taste
drive	garage	oil	upset

Write the words in the chart.

Ernesto's Job	Feelings	Actions

Explain your answers to your classmates.

ABC Vocabulary—Making the Words My Own

Finish the Sentence

Work with a partner. Find the underlined words in the journal entry. Re-read those sentences. Then finish these sentences. Write about yourself or someone you know.

When our roof started <u>leaking</u>, we _____.

I feel <u>satisfied</u> _____.

When _____, I get <u>upset</u>.

You shouldn't <u>beat someone up</u> because _____.

I never want to <u>taste</u> _____ because _____.

I repaired _____ because _____.

16 Fouad Feels Homesick

 Vocabulary Preview

alive   boil   bowl   homesick   mix   wonder

Before We Read

1. Talk about the picture. What do you see? What is happening? What do you think will happen next?

2. Talk about the title of the chapter. What do you think Fouad wrote about?

3. What do you remember about Fouad? Who is Wendy? Who is Zubair?

4. Why do you think people feel homesick? What can they do about it?

Scanning

Read Fouad's journal entry fast. Answer the question.

What is baseema? _____

Talk about your answer with a classmate.

Fouad's Journal Entry

Read the journal entry.

Dear Group,

I am happy to help Christina. Family is very important to me, too. I lost my whole family. I hope Christina finds her family.

I also enjoyed baking together at Veronica's house. I made a Sudanese dish. It's called *baseema*. It's a very sweet dessert. My mother used to make it for special holidays. When I taste it, I miss my family very much. I am still homesick.

Many of you asked me for the recipe. Here it is:

Baseema

Ingredients:

5 eggs	1 tsp of vanilla extract
1 cup confectioner's sugar	1 cup of coconut
3/4 cup butter / oil	1-1/2 cups of sugar
2 cups yogurt	1 tbsp lemon juice
2 tsp baking powder	1 cup water
2 cups flour	

1. Beat eggs and sugar. Add oil and yogurt. Mix.
2. In a separate bowl, sift flour and add baking powder and coconut. Add these to the mixture while stirring.
3. Spread mixture onto a greased tray. Bake for 30 minutes at 200° Celsius.
4. In another pan, mix sugar and lemon with water. Boil until syrup thickens.
5. When cake is cooked, pour syrup over it evenly so it soaks through.
6. Cut into squares and serve

Last week something sad happened. I looked at Wendy's family pictures again. This time I looked closely. Then I said, "Wendy, this man in the picture is not my uncle Zubair. I wanted him to be my uncle. But now I am looking closer, and I see that he really isn't my uncle." I was very disappointed. I felt alone again. Now as I am writing this, I still miss my uncle Zubair. I still miss my parents. I still miss my brothers. I wonder if they are alive somewhere.

❓ What Happened?

Mark the sentences T (true) or F (false).

_____ 1. Fouad is not homesick.

_____ 2. Fouad enjoyed baking at Veronica's house.

_____ 3. Fouad's mother made baseema every night.

_____ 4. The man in the picture was Fouad's uncle Zubair.

_____ 5. Fouad was disappointed.

Think about It

Answer the questions in a group.

1. Did cooking his mother's recipe make Fouad feel better or worse? Explain your answer.

2. Why did Fouad feel alone again?

3. Will Fouad feel homesick for the rest of his life? Why or why not?

4. Highlight or underline a sentence you like from the story. Tell why you like this sentence.

5. What might happen next?

↔ My Experiences

Discuss the questions with a partner.

1. Food makes Fouad think of his family. What food reminds you the most of home? Why?

2. What new food do you like? Why?

3. Do you sometimes feel homesick? What do you do when this happens?

 Choose one of the questions, and write about it in your journal.

Vocabulary—Working with Words

Fill in the Blanks

Complete the sentences. Use the words in the box.

| alive | boil | bowl | homesick | mix | wonder |

1. To make pancakes, mix flour and milk in a large _____.

2. _____ the sugar with the eggs.

3. Can you _____ some water for me? I'd like some tea.

4. I _____ if I will learn to speak English.

5. Oh! There's a bird lying on the ground. Is it _____?

6. Jason misses his friends. He feels _____.

Vocabulary—Making the Words My Own

Mid-Part Vocabulary Review

Look back at the words you are learning from earlier chapters. Alone, in pairs, or in groups, review these words. You might use Vocabulary Cards (page 15), Vocabulary House (page 10), or Vocabulary Challenge (page 31) to do this.

17 Christina Has Big News

Vocabulary Preview

enough   extra   have fun   hug   in-law   make money

Before We Read

1. Talk about the picture. What do you see? What is happening? What do you think will happen next?

2. Talk about the title of the chapter. What do you think Christina wrote about?

3. What do you remember about Christina? Who is Grandma Ruth?

4. What makes a family? Can a family include people who aren't related to you? Explain you answer.

5. Who is part of your family?

Scanning

Read Christina's journal entry fast. Answer the question.

Who is the baby in the picture? _____

Talk about your answer with a classmate.

Christina's Journal Entry

Read the journal entry.

Dear Group,

Thank you, thank you everyone! I really appreciate your help. Baking at Veronica's house was a lot of fun. I've never liked to bake or cook, but I had fun baking in Veronica's kitchen. I learned how to make chocolate chip cookies.

Now I have some really big news. I can hardly believe it myself. Guess what! I have an American family. That's right. Ruth Evans is my grandmother! We met downtown at Robinson's Restaurant. Right away, she hugged and kissed me. It was easy for me to hug and kiss her. I felt that I knew her. I felt close to her. She looked at me for a very long time. She looked and looked. Then she said, "You look just like your daddy. You have the same dimple in your chin. You have the same long eyelashes and the same curly hair. Look here."   **curly**—not straight

Then Grandma Ruth showed me pictures of my father. She had a lot of them. She also had a wedding picture of my mother and father. My mother looked beautiful in her wedding dress. And there was one more picture. It showed three people—a mother, a father, and a baby. Yes, you guessed it. I was that baby.

I told Grandma Ruth about the bake sale. She said, "That's wonderful, Christina. You have some very good friends. I'm happy for you. Now you also have two grandmothers. Your Baba is my daughter-in-law's mother, so she is my family, too. I will help you bring her to America. The bake sale might not make enough money. I'll add the extra money so you can go back to Bosnia and bring your other grandmother to the United States. Maybe your two grandmothers will be friends."

❓ What Happened?

Number these sentences in order.

_____ Grandma Ruth told Christina she looks like her father.

__1__ Christina met Grandma Ruth downtown.

_____ Grandma Ruth said she will help bring Baba from Bosnia.

_____ Grandma Ruth hugged and kissed Christina.

_____ Grandma Ruth showed Christina her parents' wedding photo.

_____ Christina told Grandma Ruth about the bake sale.

_____ Grandma Ruth showed Christina a picture of her with her parents.

Copy the sentences in the correct order. Write them in your notebook.

Think about It

Answer the questions in a group.

1. Why is Ruth sure that Christina is her granddaughter?

2. Why does Christina feel close to Ruth right away?

3. Which picture is most important to Christina? Why?

4. Do you think Grandma Ruth will give Christina some money to help bring Baba to Yuma? Explain your answer.

5. What might happen next?

↔ My Experiences

Look at Christina's family tree.

Christina's Family Tree

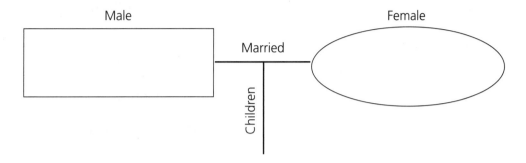

Draw your own family tree. Use these symbols. Tell about your family tree.

Discuss these questions with a group of three or four classmates. You may choose to write about one of them in your journal.

1. Do you look like someone you know? Who? How do you feel about this?

2. Were you ever surprised by something that happened to you? What happened?

3. Is there someone you want to thank? What do you want to say to them?

 Choose one of the questions, and write about it in your journal.

abc Vocabulary—Working with Words

Fill in the Blanks

Complete the sentences. Use the words in the box.

| enough   extra   have fun   hug   in-law   make money |

1. Do you have an _____ pencil? I need one for class tonight.

2. Harry doesn't want to study right now. He wants to go out and _____.

3. Grandmothers like to _____ and kiss their grandchildren.

4. Hannah's very busy. She doesn't have _____ time to work, study, and see all her friends.

5. Lee needs a job. He wants to _____ to buy a car.

6. When Alicia got married, she was happy to be in a large family. She especially liked her mother-_____.

abc Vocabulary—Making the Words My Own

Finish the Sentence

Work with a partner. Find the underlined words in the journal entry. Re-read those sentences. Then finish these sentences. Write about yourself or someone you know.

1. At the party we had <u>fun</u> when_____

2. His wife gave him a <u>hug</u> and a kiss before _____

3. When she got married, her <u>in-laws</u> _____

4. Please stop! That's <u>enough</u> _____.

5. One good way to <u>make money</u> is _____

6. Here. I have some <u>extra</u> _____. You can have some.

18 Tadeo Finds a New Home

Vocabulary Preview

> advice   community   counselor   instead of   manager   permitted

Before We Read

1. Talk about the picture. What do you see? What is happening?

2. Talk about the title of the chapter. What do you think Tadeo wrote about?

3. What do you remember about Tadeo?

4. Talk about some ways you want to change and some ways you do not want to change.

▷ Scanning

Read Tadeo's journal entry fast. Answer the question.

Where does Tadeo live now?_____

Talk about your answer with a classmate.

Tadeo's Journal Entry

Read the journal entry.

Dear Group,

I'm happy for Christina and I agree—baking at Veronica's house was wonderful. I tasted everything. I don't usually like to cook. But at Veronica's house I wanted to cook because everyone was so busy baking good things. I made simple oatmeal cookies and banana bread. Veronica told me to use honey instead of sugar for the cookies. That was a good idea. The cookies had a special taste, and they were very chewy.

I want to give Ernesto some advice. Ernesto, don't start a fight with Scott Andrews. Instead, talk to the manager of the beauty school. Scott is making Lydia feel uncomfortable. This is not permitted. The manager will stop it.

I understand why you are angry. But let me tell you something. This is a new country here. We know what to do in our home country, but here things are sometimes different. There are other things you can do. There are counselors at our school. They help people with anger. I talked to one of them about a problem I'm having, and he helped me a lot. So see a counselor. At least go one time to see if he has any ideas you like.

My news is that I now live with Eric and Carol. It feels like I have an American family. On Saturdays all three of us clean the house together. It's fun. Eric is good at cleaning the kitchen. We have two bathrooms. Carol is good at cleaning the bathrooms. I vacuum and dust the living room and all three bedrooms. Eric likes to cook so he does the cooking. Carol and I wash the dishes and put them away. Soon we will buy a dishwasher. My life is richer and fuller now that I'm living with Eric and Carol. They are my new family.

The people in this class and writing in this journal also helped me to feel much better.

❓ What Happened?

Mark these sentences (T) true or (F) false.

_____ 1. Tadeo loves to cook.

_____ 2. Tadeo made oatmeal cookies and banana bread.

_____ 3. He used sugar instead of honey.

_____ 4. Tadeo advised Ernesto to talk to the manager of Lydia's school.

_____ 5. Tadeo lives alone.

_____ 6. Tadeo cleans the house alone.

_____ 7. Carol cleans the kitchen.

_____ 8. Carol vacuums and dusts the living room and the bedrooms.

_____ 9. Eric and Carol are Tadeo's new family.

Rewrite the false sentences and make them true. Write them in your notebook.

Think about It

Answer the questions in a group.

1. Why did Tadeo advise Ernesto not to fight? What advice would you give Ernesto?

2. Did Tadeo give Ernesto good advice? Why or why not? Do you think Tadeo's grandfather would agree with this advice?

3. Why does Tadeo feel that Eric and Carol are his family now?

↔ My Experiences

Discuss the questions with a partner.

1. Tadeo talked to a counselor. Who do you talk to when you have a problem? Is there anyone else you could talk to? Do you prefer to talk with a friend, a family member, or a professional? Why?

2. Eric likes to cook. Who cooks in your home? Who cleans? Is this okay with you?

 Choose one of the questions, and write about it in your journal.

abc Vocabulary—Working with Words

Do I Know These Words?

1. Find these words in Tadeo's journal entry. Then highlight or underline them.

| advice | counselor | instead of | manager | permitted |

2. Look at each word. Ask yourself, How well do I know this word? Write one word in each row in one of the columns (A, B, C, or D).

Words	A. I don't know this word.	B. I have seen this word before.	C. I understand this word.	D. I use this word easily.
Example: party.				party
advice				
counselor				
instead of				
manager				
permitted				

3. Work with a group of three or four students. Teach your classmates about the words you know. Ask them about the words you don't know well.

4. Look at your chart again. Do you understand more words now? Which words can you move in your chart?

abc Vocabulary—Making the Words My Own

Use and Remember

1. Look at the vocabulary words in earlier chapters. Which new words are the most important for you? Write three of the words here.

_____   _____   _____

2. Work with three or four classmates. Talk about your words. Explain how you will use your words in a conversation outside of class.

3. Sit with the same students during your next class. Describe when and where you used your new words. Congratulate each other on your successes.

19 Hamad, the Proud Father

 ## Vocabulary Preview

amazed   artist   blood   information   simple   study

Before We Read

1. Talk about the picture. What do you see? What is happening?

2. Talk about the title of the chapter. What do you think Hamad wrote about?

3. What do you remember about Hamad and his sons? Who is Howard?

4. Among your family and friends, who knows more English? How do you help each other?

5. Do you use the Internet to get information? What kinds of information?

Scanning

Read Hamad's journal entry fast. Answer the question.

Who is Amanda? _____

Talk about your answer with a classmate.

Hamad's Journal Entry

Read the journal entry.

Dear Group,

I am very happy for Christina, and I agree with the advice Tadeo gave to Ernesto. Tadeo is a smart guy. I enjoy reading his journals. I can't cook or bake, but I can bring something else to our sale. I will bring some flowers and plants from my garden. I think people will want to buy them. I will even bring a camellia plant.

I had a long talk with Howard about Ali. Howard has three sons in college. He knows a lot about the schools in Yuma, and he gave me some information. He says that the gifted student program in the public schools is very good. One of his boys, Charles, was in the program. Charles is now in medical school. Howard said, "Maybe Ali wants to become a doctor."

Later I asked Ali, "Do you want to become a doctor?" Ali said, "No. I don't like to look at blood. I want to study math. It's beautiful and logical."

Ali has a lot of new friends. He doesn't miss his friends in Jordan any more. For a while he wrote e-mails to some of his old friends. But one day he said, "I can't write to Mohammed and Rami any more." "Why not? I asked. Ali answered, "I've changed too much." He seemed a little sad and confused.

Saleh has a girlfriend. Her name is Amanda. Saleh and Amanda like to help me in the garden, but Saleh doesn't want to be a gardener. He wants to study computers. He works in a computer store, and he goes to night school. Yesterday he bought a new computer. He finds a lot of gardening advice for me on the Internet. I am always amazed.

One day I said to Howard, "So much happened in my life this past year. I feel like a new man. But I am still a simple gardener. Howard laughed. "No," he said. "No, my friend. You are not a simple gardener. You are a landscape artist."

"Well," I thought. "Maybe that's true. Maybe I am a landscape artist. Anyway I am a happy man and a proud father.

❓ What Happened?

Mark these sentences (T) true or (F) false.

_____ 1. Hamad cooks and bakes.

_____ 2. Howard knows about schools in Yuma.

_____ 3. Ali wants to become a doctor.

_____ 4. Ali doesn't like to look at blood.

_____ 5. Ali still writes e-mails to his friends in Jordan.

_____ 6. Amanda is Ali's girlfriend.

_____ 7. Saleh wants to be a gardener.

Rewrite the false sentences and make them true. Write them in your notebook.

Think about It

Answer the questions in a group.

1. Why does Hamad enjoy reading Tadeo's journal?

2. Hamad says, "Ali doesn't miss his friends in Jordan." Do you think that is really true? Explain your answer.

3. Hamed says, "I am a simple gardener." Howard answers, "No, you are a landscape artist." Explain the difference.

4. Highlight or underline a sentence you like from the story. Tell why you like this sentence.

↔ My Experiences

Discuss the questions with a partner.

1. Do you make decisions for yourself? Does your family help you make important decisions? Who else helps you decide things? Explain.

2. Ali doesn't want to be a doctor. This is an easy decision for him. Ali decides not to write to Mohammed and Rami any more. This decision is difficult for him. What kinds of decisions are easy for you? What kinds of decisions are difficult? Why?

3. Is there someone who was your friend in the past but is not your friend now? Did one of you change? Explain your answer.

 Choose one of the questions. Write about it in your journal.

Vocabulary—Working with Words

Word Families

Word families help you learn a whole group of words at one time. You learned some word families in earlier chapters.

Here are some more word families.

1. Write the correct form of the words in the chart.

   amaze, amazed, amazing, amazed

   simplify, simple

   study

   information, informative

   artistic

   blood, bloody

   advise, advice, advisor

2. Write sentences. Use the words in the chart.

Adjective	Noun	Verb	Adverb
	amazement		————
	————		simply
————	student	..	————
————		inform, informed	————
	artist, art	————	————
		bleed	————
————	advice, _____		————

3. Work with a classmate. Read your sentences, and listen to their sentences. Compare them.

Vocabulary—Making the Words My Own

Vocabulary House

1. Look again at page 10. Then take out your Vocabulary House. In small groups, talk about the words in each room. Tell why you put those words there.

2. Choose new words you want to remember. Decide where to write them in your Vocabulary House, and tell your group why.

Vocabulary Challenge

Look at the six words in Vocabulary Preview. How many of them can you use in one sentence? Share your sentence with the class.

Part 3 Checklist: How Did I Do?

Think about the things you did as you worked through Unit 3.
Check the things you did.

_____ I worked with a partner or a group.

_____ I asked questions when I didn't understand something.

_____ I wrote journal entries.

_____ I made vocabulary cards.

_____ I added words to my Vocabulary House.

_____ I used new vocabulary in and out of class.

_____ I read the stories once without using my dictionary.

_____ I used a highlighter to highlight important words or sentences in the journals.

_____ I reviewed what we studied in class when I went home.

What things do you want to try that you didn't do? Write one or two ideas that you will try in the next unit.

_____

_____

Share your answers with two or three classmates.

Veronica's Last Letter

Scanning

Read Veronica's letter fast. Answer the question.

How much money did they make for the bake sale? _____

Talk about your answer with a classmate.

Veronica's Letter

Read the letter.

Dear Students,

I really enjoyed your last journals. I loved having you in my house. I will miss all of you very much, and I hope some of you continue to write. Please e-mail me all your news.

Last night Lydia, Adriana, and I counted all the money we made from our bake and plant sale. We made $245.58. That's a lot of money, but it's not enough to send Christina to Bosnia and bring her grandmother with her to the United States. I'm glad that Mrs. Evans will help Christina with the rest of the money.

I also want to thank Tadeo. He wrote something very important in his last journal.

He wrote about the counseling office in our school. The counselors are very helpful. They talk to people about their problems, and they can help if you feel lonely, frightened, sad, or angry. It's always good to talk to another person. The counselors never tell anyone else what they hear. They never talk about the people who come to them. They are professionals. They know how to help.

I look forward to reading more in your journals.

Warm regards to everyone,

Veronica

Think about It

What do you think will happen in Part 4?

20 Lydia Solves Her Problem

connected	encourage	in style	sew	success	vegetarian

Before We Read

1. Talk about the picture. What do you see? What is happening?

2. Talk about the title of the chapter. What do you think Lydia wrote about?

3. What do you remember about Lydia? Who is Scott Andrews?

4. Talk about a meal you enjoyed with other people.

▷ Scanning

Read Lydia's journal entry fast. Answer the question.

What do the boys like to eat? _____

Talk about your answer with a classmate.

Lydia's Journal Entry

Read the journal entry.

Dear Group,

It was such an exciting week. The bake sale was a great success. It's wonderful that Veronica opened her house to us. I enjoyed meeting Ruth, Christina's American grandmother, at the bake sale. She sews many of her own clothes and she sells others in her store in Minneapolis. She wears clothes that are in style. I loved her black skirt and her orange blouse.

Grandma Ruth and Adriana's Aunt Teresa got along very well. Aunt Teresa invited Christina and Ruth to dinner with us next Saturday. Adriana and I are planning this dinner very carefully because Ruth is a vegetarian. She doesn't eat meat. We plan to make a dish with rice and vegetables like squash, carrots, and beans. We are also planning a large salad with spinach, tomatoes, cucumbers, radishes, and onions. I love onions. I put them in almost every dish I cook, just like my mother does.

Fouad and Ernesto are coming to dinner too, and we will make a meat dish for them. We might make lamb stew. The boys really like that.

We are all connected. We are connected not just to people who live now. We are connected to all the people who lived before us, too.

Something else happened this week. Ernesto encouraged me to talk with Mrs. Villegas, the director of our beauty school. So I told her what was happening. Guess what? Scott Andrews doesn't bother me any more!

? What Happened?

Work with a partner. Answer the questions.

1. How was the bake sale? _____

2. What did Lydia admire about Christina's Grandma Ruth? _____

3. Do Christina's Grandma Ruth and Lydia's Aunt Teresa like each other? _____

4. Who did Aunt Teresa invite to dinner? _____

5. Why does Lydia have to plan this dinner carefully? _____

6. Why does Lydia like to use a lot of onions when she cooks? _____

7. Who is Mrs. Villegas? _____

8. Why did Lydia talk with her? _____

Think about It

Answer the questions in a group.

1. Do you think Veronica is a good teacher? Why or why not?

2. Why do the girls make a special dish for Fouad and Ernesto? Is this necessary?

3. What did Mrs. Villegas do?

4. What might happen next?

↔ My Experiences

Discuss the questions with a partner.

1. Christina and her mother use a lot of onions when they cook. What connections do you see between you and the people who came before you?

2. Do you like to cook or sew? Explain your answers.

3. Are the right kinds of clothes important to you? Why or why not?

4. Do you like to shop? Why or why not?

 Choose one of the questions, and write about it in your journal.

Vocabulary—Working with Words

Match

Match the words with their meanings.

___e___ 1. sew

a. a person who doesn't eat meat

_____ 2. vegetarian

b. say, "You can do it"

_____ 3. connected

c. good result

_____ 4. encourage

d. having clothes that are in fashion

_____ 5. success

e. make clothes

_____ 6. in style

f. joined/close to

Categories

Read the words in the box. Then put them in the correct column in the chart.

beans	lamb stew	onions	spinach
carrots	meat	radishes	squash
cucumbers	noodles	salad	tomatoes

foods I like	foods I don't like

Add some more foods! Talk with some classmates about foods you like and don't like.

Vocabulary—Making the Words My Own

Finish the Sentence

Work with a partner. Find the underlined words in the journal entry. Re-read those sentences. Then finish these sentences. Write about yourself or someone you know.

connected	encourage	in style	sew	success	vegetarian

1. I feel <u>connected</u> with _____.

2. Sometimes it is important to be <u>in style</u>. For example, _____.

3. Some people like to <u>sew</u> because _____.

4. I <u>encouraged</u> _____ to _____.

5. _____'s big <u>success</u> was _____.

6. Some people are <u>vegetarians</u> because _____.

21 Ernesto's New Car

 ## Vocabulary Preview

appointment   changing   a good deal   regular   sell   worth

Before We Read

1. Talk about the picture. What do you see? What is happening?

2. Talk about the title of the chapter. What do you think Ernesto wrote about?

3. What do you remember about Ernesto?

4. Talk about the last thing you bought.

5. Talk about something you own and why it is important to you.

Scanning

Read Ernesto's journal entry fast. Answer the question.

What color is Ernesto's new car? _____

Talk about your answer with a classmate.

Ernesto's Journal Entry

Read the journal entry.

Dear Group,

I took Tadeo's advice and made an appointment with a counselor at school. His name is Jim. Lydia and I saw him twice last week. He was very helpful. Later Lydia talked to Mrs. Villegas, the director of her beauty school. That did it! Nobody bothers Lydia now. I want to talk some more with Jim. I learned something very important—quiet talk works better than anger. Knowing this helps me at work, too.

It was a great week for me. Yesterday I bought my first car! One day Mr. Hajjar brought his car in. He's an older man, one of our regular customers. While I was changing the oil in his car, Mr. Hajjar said, "This is my wife's car, but now she's sick and can't drive it any more. So I have to sell it. I need to write an ad for the Internet, but I don't like to write!"

I said, "I understand, Mr. Hajjar. I didn't like to write either. But in my writing course we write journals every week. Now I am beginning to like writing." Then I asked him, "How much do you want for this car?" "The car is worth a lot," he answered, "but I'll take less because I want to sell it fast." "Maybe I can buy your car," I said. Mr. Hajjar answered, "Ernesto, I am going to give you a good deal, and you can pay a little every month."

Mr. Hajjar sold the car to me for a very good price. It's a white Buick with automatic transmission and brand new tires. It drives beautifully. It looks like it's new. I love it, and Lydia loves it, too. Now I have a beautiful car.

Veronica, this has been a wonderful class. I want to thank you and all of my classmates for your help. Someday Lydia and I will get married. If we have a daughter, we will call her Veronica.

? What Happened?

Number the sentences in order

___1___ Ernesto made an appointment with a counselor.

_____ Ernesto wanted to buy the car from Mr. Hajjar.

_____ Ernesto thanked Veronica for her help.

_____ Lydia talked to Mrs. Villegas.

_____ Mr. Hajjar decided to sell his wife's car.

_____ Mr. Hajjar's wife got sick.

_____ Mr. Hajjar needed to write an ad.

_____ Ernesto saw the counselor two times.

_____ Ernesto bought his first American car.

Copy the sentences in the correct order. Write them in your notebook.

Think about It

Answer the questions in a group.

1. Why did Ernesto offer to write an ad for Mr. Hajjar?

2. Is Mr. Hajjar really giving Ernesto a good deal?

3. Why is Ernesto so happy with his new car?

4. What are some of the ways that Veronica and Ernesto's classmates have helped him?

5. What might happen next?

↔ My Experiences

Discuss the questions with a partner.

1. Ernesto bought a car. Think of something you bought. Why did you buy it? Are you happy with this purchase?

2. Is bargaining easy or difficult for you? Why? When and where can you bargain in the United States?

  Choose one of the questions and write about it in your journal.

ᵃᵇᶜ Vocabulary—Working with Words

Do I Know These Words?

1. Find the words and phrases in Ernesto's journal entry. Then highlight or underline them.

appointment sell change a good deal regular worth

2. Look at each word. Ask yourself, How well do I know this word? Write one word in each row in one of the columns (A, B, C, or D).

Words	A. I don't know this word.	B. I have seen this word before.	C. I understand this word.	D. I use this word easily.
Example: party.				*party*
appointment				
sell				
change				
a good deal				
rregular				
worth				

3. Work with a group of three or four students. Teach your classmates about the words you know. Ask them about the words you don't know well.

4. Look at your chart again. Do you understand more words now? Which words can you move in your chart?

ᵃᵇᶜ Vocabulary—Making the Words My Own

Vocabulary Cards

Look again at page 15. Review your Vocabulary Cards. Make five new ones.

22 Fouad Finds Family

 Vocabulary Preview

courage   dentist   disappointed   invited   operation   recommend

 Before We Read

1. Talk about the picture. What do you see? What is happening? What do you think will happen next?

2. Talk about the title of the article. What do you think Fouad wrote about?

3. What do you remember about Fouad? How is Wendy part of his life?

4. Talk about some people who are new in your life this year. What do you do together?

▷ **Scanning**

Read Fouad's journal entry fast. Answer the question.

Why is Fouad disappointed? _____

Talk about your answer with a classmate.

Fouad's Journal Entry

Read the journal entry.

I really enjoy having dinner on Saturday with Ernesto at his Aunt Teresa's house. This week Wendy is invited, too. Wendy is now a large part of my life. We go to the movies together. We have lunch together every Wednesday and Friday. We read and talk about books a lot. Wendy recommends books to me all the time, and she always keeps new books in the library for me. I like to do my homework in the library while I wait for Wendy.

Last week I got a part-time job at the library. I put books back on the shelves. I put up posters, and I'm learning how to find information on the computer. I want to help the people who need information. I want to make people feel at home in the library. The library was a big help to me. Now I want to help other people.

Yesterday a woman came to the library. She needed information about eye operations. Her doctor said she needs an operation and she was afraid. I helped her find the information, and I talked with her.

She said, "Fouad, you are a very nice young man. I was afraid of the operation, but you gave me courage. You found good information for me. I feel safer now because I understand what this operation is about."

I was disappointed at first because the man in Wendy's picture was not my Uncle Zubair. But I have met him, and I like him. He is from Sudan too, and we talk about our country. We can be homesick together.

Veronica, I just remembered that you are moving to a new city. You asked for our advice. I hope you find the library. I hope you find a good place to live, a good doctor, and a good dentist. Those are all important. You also need a supermarket. You and your husband can get all kinds of information about Tucson on the Internet. I am happy to help.

❓ What Happened?

Work with a partner. Answer the questions.

1. What did Fouad do last Saturday? _____

2. What do Wendy and Fouad do together every week? _____

3. What happened last week? _____

4. What does Fouad do in the library? _____

5. What happened yesterday? _____

6. Why is the woman less afraid now? _____

7. Why was Fouad disappointed? _____

8. Why does Fouad like the man from Sudan? _____

9. What advice does he give Veronica? _____

Copy the sentences in your notebook.

Think about It

Answer the questions in a group.

1. How has Fouad's and Wendy's relationship changed and developed?

2. Highlight or <u>underline</u> a sentence that you liked in the journal. Tell why you liked it.

3. Is the job in the library a good one for Fouad? Why or why not?

4. What might happen next?

⟷ My Experiences

Discuss the questions with a partner.

1. Veronica might look for information about Tucson on the Internet. Have you found a good doctor, dentist, supermarket, restaurant, bank, post office, or other useful place? How did you find them?

2. Is there someone you haven't talked with recently? What do you want to tell them?

3. Have you ever felt disappointed? What happened?

4. Fouad found someone from his culture to talk with when he is homesick. Do you have someone you can talk to? How do you help each other?

 Choose one of the questions and write about it in your journal.

ꭈᑲᶜ Vocabulary—Working with Words

Fill in the Blanks

Complete the sentences. Use the words in the box.

courage	dentist	disappointed	invited	operation	recommend

1. When you are afraid, you need _____.

2. I read a good book. I _____ it to all my friends.

3. After Joe's _____, he felt better.

4. Diana went to the store for chocolate ice cream, but they didn't have any. She was

   _____.

5. Paulo's tooth hurt, so he went to the _____.

6. I _____ all my friends to my party last month.

abc Vocabulary—Making the Words My Own

Practice with the Word Recommend

Write about four things that you recommend.

I **recommend** J and J Supermarket because the fruit is always fresh.

a. Book _____

b. Movie _____

c. Restaurant _____

d. Store _____

Walk around the class, and make recommendations to your classmates.

Mid-Part Vocabulary Review

Look back at the words you are learning from Chapters 20–22. Alone, in pairs, or in groups, review these words. You might use Vocabulary Cards (page 15), Vocabulary House (page 10), or Vocabulary Challenge (page 31) to do this.

23 Christina's Big Family

"Je li stvarno ćeš doć? Stvarno?"

 ## Vocabulary Preview

miracle   plan   relative   return   reunion   village

 ## Before We Read

1. Talk about the picture. What do you see? What is happening? What do you think will happen next?

2. Talk about the title of the chapter. What do you think Christina wrote about?

3. What do you remember about Christina?

4. Is there someone who lives far away that you would like to bring here? Who? Why?

▷ Scanning

Read Christina's journal entry fast. Answer the question.

Who has a big house? _____

Talk about your answer with a classmate.

Christina's Journal Entry

Read the journal entry.

Well, believe it or not, I am going back to Bosnia at the end of this month. Baba is meeting me at the airport in Sarajevo. A woman from my church group is bringing her from our village. They got a visa for her. Last night I talked with Baba on the phone. She is so excited. She said, "Is it really you, Christina? Are you really coming to get me? Maybe I am just dreaming. Can you really speak English now? Do you really have an American grandmother? Are you coming to get me? Are you really coming?"

We talked and talked. I cried and Baba cried. I told her about the bake sale. Baba said, "How wonderful. What a miracle. What wonderful people." Baba can't wait to see me, and I can't wait to see her.

Grandma Ruth is excited, too. She said, "Christina, when you and Baba return, would you like to plan a big party and invite all of your classmates? And would you and Baba like to come with me to Minneapolis? I have a big house, and we can all live there together. You've got a lot of American relatives in Minneapolis. They are all waiting to meet you! It will be a family reunion." And I need more help in my store. Would you like to work there?

I hope that Grandma Ruth and Baba like each other. I love both of them.

❓ What Happened?

Mark these sentences (T) true or (F) false.

___F___ 1. Christina is going to Paris at the end of the month.

_____ 2. She is traveling to her grandmother's small town.

_____ 3. Baba is meeting Christina at the airport.

_____ 4. Baba is excited.

_____ 5. Baba is just dreaming.

_____ 6. Grandma Ruth wants to have a big party.

_____ 7. Christina might work in Grandma Ruth's store.

Re-write the false sentences and make them true. Write them in your notebook.

Think about It

Answer the questions in a group.

1. Why did Baba say, "Maybe I am just dreaming."

2. Why did Baba say, "What a miracle!"? Do you agree with her?

3. Why did Grandma Ruth invite Christina to work in her store?

4. Do you think Christina's grandmothers will like each other? Why or why not?

5. What might happen next?

↔ My Experiences

Discuss the questions with a partner.

1. Christina's Grandma Ruth is planning a party. Do you like parties? What makes a good party?

2. Imagine that you're planning a party. What are you going to do? Consider people, place, food, entertainment, etc.

3. A friend is moving to the United States. What advice can you give to him or her to make adjusting easier?

4. Were you ever reunited with someone from your past? What happened?

 Choose one of the questions and write about it in your journal.

abc Vocabulary—Working with Words

Do I Know These Words?

1. Find these words in Christina's journal entry. Then highlight or underline them.

miracle	plan	relative	return	reunion	village

2. Look at each word. Ask yourself, How well do I know this word? Write one word in each row in one of the columns (A, B, C, or D).

Words	A. I don't know this word.	B. I have seen this word before.	C. I understand this word.	D. I use this word easily.
Example: party.				party
miracle				
plan				
relative				
return				
reunion				
village				

3. Work with a group of three or four students. Teach your classmates about the words you know. Ask them about the words you don't know well.

4. Look at your chart again. Do you understand more words now? Which words can you move in your chart?

Vocabulary—Making the Words My Own

Finish the Sentence

Work with a partner. Find the underlined words in the journal entry. Re-read those sentences. Then finish these sentences. Write about yourself or someone you know.

1. My <u>plan</u> for next year is to _____

2. A <u>miracle</u> happened when _____ .

3. _____ is my favorite <u>relative</u> because _____ .

4. We went to the <u>reunion</u> and saw _____

5. Sometimes it isn't easy to <u>return</u> home _____ .

6. In the <u>village</u>, _____

24 Tadeo's New Family

 Vocabulary Preview

approve of   discovered   driver's license   passed   spirit   trouble

 Before We Read

1. Talk about the picture. What do you see? What is happening? What do you think will happen next?

2. Talk about the title of the chapter. What do you think Tadeo wrote about?

3. What do you remember about Tadeo?

4. Do you ever think about your relatives who lived before you? Explain.

▷ **Scanning**

Read Tadeo's journal entry fast. Answer the question.

What is the dog's name?_____

Talk about your answer with a partner.

Tadeo's Journal Entry

Read the journal entry.

Dear Group,

Several interesting things happened last week. I passed my driving test and got my driver's license. Now I can drive Carol to school in Eric's car. This is a big help for Eric. Soon I am going to get my own car. I really enjoy driving around Yuma. I discovered some interesting new neighborhoods. We also got a dog. Carol has always wanted a dog, but Eric said, "A dog is too much trouble."

I agree with Carol. I love dogs, too. I've always wanted a dog, but my parents were just like Eric.

One day Carol and I went to the Humane Society. There were a lot of dogs in cages. They looked very sad. One little cocker spaniel looked and looked at Carol and me. The little dog put its nose against Carol's hand. I thought, "This dog wants to come home with us. He is saying, 'You came to get me, didn't you?'" Carol looked at me and I looked at Carol. Both of us looked at the cocker spaniel. Then Carol said, "I think he wants to come home with us. I think his name is Sandy."

cages—boxes with metal bars that people sometimes keep animals in

Sandy came home with us. Eric said, "You two have to take care of him. I don't have time." So Carol and I take care of Sandy. Carol takes him for a walk every morning. I take him for a walk at night. I bought the food for Sandy, and I gave him a bath. Sandy is always happy to see me when I come home. I like that. Sandy is good company.

Like everyone else in the class, I am very happy about Christina's grandmother. Let's all go to the airport to meet Christina and her grandmother.

I often think about my grandfather. Sometimes when I walk in the park with Eric, Carol, and Sandy, I think that my grandfather's spirit is next to me. I think my grandfather would approve of my life in the United States.

spirit—a "ghost"

What Happened?

Number the sentences in order.

_____ Tadeo and Carol brought Sandy home.

___1___ Tadeo got his driver's license.

_____ Tadeo thinks about his grandfather.

_____ Tadeo gave Sandy a bath.

_____ Tadeo and Carol found a dog.

In your notebook, copy the sentences in the correct order.

Think about It

Answer the questions in a group.

1. Why doesn't Eric want a dog? Why do you think Tadeo and Carol get a dog anyway?

2. How does Tadeo know that Sandy is always happy to see him when he comes home?

3. What are some things Tadeo might do now that he has a driver's license?

4. What might happen next?

5. Do you think Tadeo's grandfather would approve of Tadeo's life in the United States. Why or why not?

↔ My Experiences

Discuss the questions.

1. Tadeo got a driver's license. Do you have a driver's license? If not, do you want one? Why or why not?

2. Do you have a pet? If not, do you want one? Why do you think people enjoy having pets?

3. Did you have a pet when you were young? What kind? If not, did you want one?

 Choose one of the questions, and write about it in your journal.

abc Vocabulary—Working with Words

Fill in the Blanks

Complete the sentences. Use the words in the box.

approve of	bath	discovered	driver's license	passed	trouble

1. Andres got his _____. Now he can go anywhere he wants to go.

2. Grace bought an expensive sports car. Her parents don't _____ her decision.

3. We _____ a great Chinese restaurant last night.

4. I studied very hard so I was very happy that I _____ the test.

5. The baby didn't cry all night. She was no _____.

6. Ivanka doesn't like to take showers. She always takes a _____.

abc Vocabulary—Making the Words My Own

Use and Remember

1. Look at the vocabulary words in earlier chapters. Which new words are the most important for you? Write three of the words here.

   _____   _____   _____

2. Work with three or four classmates. Talk about your words. Explain how you will use your words in a conversation outside of class.

3. Sit with the same students during your next class. Describe when and where you used your new words. Congratulate each other on your success.

25 Hamad Gets a Surprise Phone Call

Vocabulary Preview

contest   essay   message   publish   website   win

Before We Read

1. Talk about the picture. What do you see? What is happening? What do you think will happen next?

2. Talk about the title of the chapter. What do you think Hamad wrote about?

3. What do you remember about Hamad and his sons?

4. What are your dreams for the future?

▷ Scanning

Read Hamad's journal entry fast. Answer the question.

What did Henry Larson say in his message? _____

Talk about your answer with a classmate.

Hamad's Journal Entry

Read the journal entry.

Dear Group,

I was happy to sell so many of my plants during the bake sale. It is wonderful that Christina now has two grandmothers. I want to take flowers to the airport for both grandmothers.

I heard that in the United States many children don't listen to their parents. I was worried about my boys, but that hasn't happened. My boys are very good. I think about my wife a lot these days. If she were alive, she would be proud of our boys. Now I am thinking that maybe my sister Aisha can come and live with us.

This past week Ali won an essay contest. He read his essay to me. It was about gardens. It was very beautiful, but I didn't understand all of it. It was published in the newspaper with Ali's picture. I showed the newspaper to Veronica, and she will read it to the whole class. She wants Ali to come and talk to us.

Saleh built a website for me. It has beautiful pictures of my flowers. I am very proud of both my boys. The boys say, "After we go to college and make some money, we will help you start a landscaping business." It is a dream, but who knows?

Yesterday I got a message from a man from New York City. He said, "Mr. Al-Thani, my name is Henry Larson. I saw your website, and I am interested in working with you."

I don't know what he wants. Who knows what might happen?

What Happened?

Answer the questions with your group.

1. What is Hamad going to the airport for? _____

2. Why was Hamad worried about his boys?_____

3. Who might come to United States? _____

4. Why was Ali's picture in the newspaper?_____

5. How did Saleh help his father? _____

6. What is Hamad's dream? _____

7. Why did Henry Larson call Hamad? _____

Think about It

1. Why is Hamad proud of his boys? How do Hamad's boys help him?

2. Christina is bringing her grandmother to United States. Hamad might bring his sister. Which other students in Veronica's class do you think will bring family members here?

3. Highlight or underline a sentence you like from the story. Tell why you like this sentence.

4. What might happen next?

↔ My Experiences

Discuss the questions.

1. Hamad's sons are making plans. What are your goals, dreams, and plans for the future?

2. What are some problems that young people face today?

 Choose one of the questions, and write about it in your journal.

abc Vocabulary—Working with Words

Fill in the Blanks

Complete the sentences. Use the words in the box.

contest	essay	message	published	website	win

1. Victoria had to write an _____ about her life for her English class.

2. Her teacher _____ her essay in the school newspaper.

3. She also published it on the school _____. Now people all over the world can read Victoria's essay!

4. In every _____, there are winners and losers.

5. If I _____ the lottery, I will use the money to help my family.

6. No one was home when Patrick called, so he left a _____.

abc Vocabulary—Making the Words My Own

Vocabulary House

1. Look again at page 10. Take out your Vocabulary House. In small groups, talk about the words in each room. Tell why you put those words there.

2. Choose new words you want to remember. Decide where to write them in your Vocabulary House, and tell your group why.

Part 4 Checklist: How Did I Do?

Think about the things you did as you worked through Part 4.
Check the things you did.

_____ I worked with a partner or a group.

_____ I asked questions when I didn't understand something.

_____ I wrote journal entries.

_____ I made vocabulary cards.

_____ I added words to my Vocabulary House.

_____ I used new vocabulary in and out of class.

_____ I read the stories once without using my dictionary.

_____ I used a highlighter to highlight important words or sentences in the journals.

_____ I reviewed what we studied in class when I went home.

What things do you want to try that you didn't do? Write one or two ideas that you will try in the future.

_____

_____

Share your answers with two or three classmates.

Conclusion

Veronica's Last Letter

 ## Scanning

Read Veronica's letter fast. Answer the question.

Who is looking for a new roommate? _____

Talk about your answer with a classmate.

Veronica's Letter

Read the letter.

Dear Group,

   It was wonderful to be at the airport with all of you. I can still see Christina's shining face. She was happy to see all of us there. Her Bosnian grandmother looked tired but very happy. When the two grandmothers hugged each other, I thought, "They will be good friends." Hamad's flowers were perfect.

   Some of you are moving to different places. But many of you are staying in Yuma. I am going to Tucson. Christina and her two grandmothers are going to Minneapolis. Adriana is moving back to San Diego. She already has a job there. Lydia and Ernesto are also going back to San Diego. They will get married there. Then they are coming back to Yuma. Tadeo is living with Eric and Carol and will stay here; Yuma is his home now. Hamad and his sons are staying in Yuma, but who knows what the future will bring? I guess Fouad is looking for a new roommate until he and Wendy get married. Congratulations on your engagement, Fouad!

Everybody learned so much English. I am proud of all of you, and I wish you many more successes. May you go from strength to strength. I will miss you all. Let's keep in touch. You have my e-mail address.

Veronica

 # Think about It

What do you think will happen next?

Appendixes

Looking Back and Looking Forward

On your own, think about these questions. Choose one question and write about it on a separate sheet of paper. Your teacher will set a time limit.

1. How did each of the students in this writing group "find family"?

2. Pretend you are one of the students from Veronica's class, and it is one year later. Write an email to Veronica. (For example, you are Ernesto or Lydia. You have a daughter and name her Veronica . . . .)

3. Write about three times in your life you were lucky or unlucky.

4. Imagine your life five years from now. Where will you be? What will you be doing?

In groups of four to five students, talk about what you have written.

Tape your own written work on the walls around the room. Walk around the room. Read the work of other students. Write positive comments on their papers.

With the whole class, talk about something from another student's paper that you liked.

Note Taking: Remembering the People and the Stories

This is a place to take notes. As you go through the book, write the names of new people in each chapter and how they are related to Veronica or one of her six students. Also, decide what you think are the most important things that happened in each chapter. You may do this alone or with a partner. You can look back at the stories if you need help.

Why is note-taking a good idea? There are several reasons:

- Choosing which events are the most important will help you understand the story. It is also a good way to begin writing summaries.
- Taking notes here will help you remember what you read.

- Sometimes one of your classmates may miss a class or forget what happened in a chapter. You can talk to each other about your notes in this section and help them catch up.
- You can work in small groups to talk about what each of you wrote and why. Different people often have different ideas about what was most important.

Characters	New people and their relationship to the character	Most important things that happened to this character
Veronica	Amelia, her childhood friend her parents Mrs. Bledowski, her teacher	— was afraid in school because she didn't speak English — felt bad about her house — her teacher helped her
Lydia		
Ernesto		

Fouad		
Christina		
Tadeo		
Hamad		

Preview of Words by Chapter

Part 1

No preview words

1. afraid   grade   look forward to   parents   repeat   toys
2. angry   fight   grow up   neighbor   (be) sorry   stupid
3. clerk   confused   jealous   move in   tell a lie   wake up / woke up
4. attacked   government   library/librarian   lose/lost   safe   shout
5. accident   believe   find out about   glad   remember   turning point
6. divide   enemy   fold   probably   protect   survived
7. admire   business   expert   garden   treasure   trip

Part 2

8. clean   forgive   invite   lonely   right away   spoil
9. definitely   follow her heart   insisted   leave home   make plans   take care of
10. explain   prefer   touch   sour   sweet   unlucky
11. busy   customers   package   proud   tips   worried (about)
12. during   nurse   patients   sadness   visit   volunteer
13. gifted   lazy   principal   (in a state of) shock   smart   special

Part 3

14. delicious   delighted   disappear   funny   suggestion   uncomfortable
15. beat someone up   leak   repair   taste   satisfied   upset
16. alive   boil   bowl   homesick   mix   wonder
17. enough   extra   have fun   hug   in-law   make money
18. advice   community   counselor   instead (of)   manager   permitted
19. amazed   artist   blood   information   simple   study

Part 4

20. connected   encourage   in style   sew   success   vegetarian
21. appointment   changing   a good deal   regular   sell   worth
22. courage   dentist   disappointed   invited   operation   recommend
23. miracle   plan   relative   return   reunion   village
24. approve of   discovered   driver's license   passed   spirit   trouble
25. contest   essay   message   publish   website   win

Common Irregular Verbs

Plain Form	Past	Past Participle	Plain Form	Past	Past Participle
be	was/were	been	let	let	let
become	became	become	lie	lay	laid
begin	began	begun	lose	lost	lost
bend	bent	bent	make	made	made
bite	bit	bitten	mean	meant	meant
bleed	bled	bled	meet	met	met
break	broke	broken	pay	paid	paid
bring	brought	brought	put	put	put
build	built	built	read	read	read
buy	bought	bought	ride	rode	ridden
catch	caught	caught	rise	rose	risen
choose	chose	chosen	run	ran	run
come	came	come	say	said	said
cost	cost	cost	see	saw	seen
creep	crept	crept	send	sent	sent
cut	cut	cut	set	set	set
dig	dug	dug	sing	sang	sung
dive	dove	dived	sink	sank	sunk
do	did	done	sit	sat	sat
draw	drew	drawn	slide	slid	slid
drink	drank	drunk	speak	spoke	spoken
drive	drove	driven	spin	spun	spun
fall	fell	fallen	spit	spit	spit
feed	fed	fed	stand	stood	stood
feel	felt	felt	sting	stung	stung
fight	fought	fought	swear	swore	sworn
find	found	found	sweep	swept	swept
forbid	forbade	forbidden	swim	swam	swum
forgive	forgave	forgiven	take	took	taken
freeze	froze	frozen	teach	taught	taught
get	got	gotten	tell	told	told
give	gave	given	think	thought	thought
go	went	gone	throw	threw	thrown
grind	ground	ground	understand	understood	understood
grow	grew	grown	wake	woke	woken
have	had	had	wear	wore	worn
hear	heard	heard	weave	wove	woven
hit	hit	hit	win	won	won
hold	held	held	write	wrote	written
hurt	hurt	hurt			
keep	kept	kept			
know	knew	known			
lay	laid	lain			
lead	led	led			
leave	left	left			